I am extraordinarily impressed with this books' scope and quality. It is thoughtfully put together, practical, honest, Biblically grounded with Biblical insights presented in such a way as to make them attractively appealing. In these chapters I see Dale Perkins shining through, the irrepressible, unpredictable, unabashed, always forward looking, Dale Perkins. With this book Dale is serving the Lord with great zeal and effectiveness.

—Dr. Thomas Price, Jr.
Prominent Methodist Minister in the State of Florida

Dale has a unique gift of weaving stories and painting observations about Scripture in a way that challenges us to explore new perspectives and insights, while staying true to the essence of its meaning. He not only takes us on a journey of a life in faith, knowing Dale, he lives it out in his own life.

—Rev. Gary Rideout
First United Methodist Winter Park

The best interpreters of Scripture allow the Bible to describe the world as God desires it to be and simply invite others on a journey into this world. In *Looking at Life Through God-Colored Glasses*, Dale Perkins brings the message of the Gospel to life. He leads his readers through the grand narrative of the Scriptures by skillfully moving between the ancient text and the challenges of modern world. His writing is colorful and enriched by well-chosen illustrations and metaphors drawn from a wide array of life experiences. I recommend this book highly. It will lead you closer to the God of the Bible—the God who loves you immensely.

—Brian D. Russell, Ph.D.
Professor of Biblical Studies, Asbury Theological Seminary

D0927091

I learned a lot...folksy, humorous,
  conversational, intellectual,
    thought-provoking, shines to faith,
      deeply thought out.
        Overall?...WOW!
                              —Mrs. Susan Goff

Whether you are a new believer or a veteran in the faith, this book affirms over and over the relevance of Scripture today. Dale has done a beautiful job giving story to biblical truths and helping us all apply them to our lives.
                              —Rev. Jayne Rideout
                    First United Methodist Winter Park

LOOKING AT LIFE THROUGH GOD-COLORED GLASSES

LOOKING AT LIFE
T H R O U G H
GOD-COLORED
G L A S S E S

DISCOVERING **THE KEY** TO ALL THAT GOD HAS FOR YOU

R. DALE PERKINS

Oviedo, Florida

Looking at Life Through God-Colored Glasses: Discovering the Key to All That God Has for You
by R. Dale Perkins

Published by HigherLife Development Services, Inc.
400 Fontana Circle
Building 1 – Suite 105
Oviedo, Florida 32765
(407) 563-4806
www.ahigherlife.com

Unless otherwise identified, Scripture quotations are from the King James Version (KJV) of the Bible.

Scripture quotations marked AMP are taken from the Amplified Bible, Copyright © 1954, 1958, 1962, 1964, 1965, 1987 by The Lockman Foundation. (www.Lockman.org).

ISBN 13: 978-1-935245-32-2
ISBN 10: 1-935245-32-5

Cover Design: Judy McKittrick Wright

10 11 12 13 — 9 8 7 6 5 4 3 2

Printed in the United States of America

CONTENTS

ACKNOWLEDGMENTS

THIS BOOK HAS been a long time coming, and there are a great many people who have had a hand in its creation. There are those who have prompted and challenged me to finish it, and without them its completion would not have been possible.

First and foremost, there is my dear wife, Sara, who continually fanned the flames that burned deep within me to renew and build on the faith that she knew lay hidden. She physically took me by the hand and led me to the doorstep of the church, and she had the presence of mind to let me figure it all out for myself. For that I will always be grateful.

Then there is my dear friend, counselor, minister, fellow world traveler, Dr. Thomas Price Jr., through whom I have learned so much about how God would have us live. Dr. Price has allowed me to glean from his personal research, knowledge, sermons, and writings to attempt to put into practical, everyday terms, answers to those questions we all ask. Dr. Price has not only helped in showing me the way to live, but he has also shown me the way to endure the pain of the loss of loved ones. His wisdom, intelligence, and encyclopedic knowledge are both amazing and indispensable. I will be ETERNALLY grateful.

A special thank-you to Dr. Joel Hunter, senior pastor of Northland, A Church Distributed, for his generous contribution of allowing me to use excerpts from his sermons in the writing of this book.

I wish to extend my most sincere appreciation to Donna Sue Armstrong for her perseverance, tenacity, and expertise in the editing of this manuscript. If you're not careful, you just might mistake Donna Sue for Ms. Laird in chapter 27, "The Faith of Another." Thank you, Donna Sue.

Through my personal reading, I am indebted to many great Christian authors—C. S. Lewis, Max Lucado, Tim LaHaye, Pat Morley, J. Vernon McGee, John Eldredge, and on and on—who have gone before this feeble attempt of mine. It should be apparent any reference of their work cannot be exact. Any mistakes of quotes that are made are due to memory, age, and pure laziness on my part, not theirs.

To my children and grandchildren and any who so desire to read this book, this assembly of writings has been written, compiled, and used by me in countless disciple classes, missionary trips throughout Central America, Walk to

Emmaus, Promise Keepers, and other Christian functions I have been involved with through the years in an attempt to give glory to God.

I do not suppose myself remotely qualified to instructively interpret Scripture, nor can I claim divine assistance but can only offer to the reader my personal observation and understanding of what I have read, which brings solace to an inquisitive, troubled, searching soul.

My only ambition and prayer is to bring to you, in the most humble way, an untrained attempt at clarity of the Scriptures and a deeper understanding of God's love mingled with an attempt at humor.

Blessings,
Dale

INTRODUCTION

O N MAY 5, 1992, at 3:30 p.m., I received the call that every parent dreads ever having to face. My fifteen-year-old son Ryan had been involved in an automobile accident. I picked up my wife Sara from the school where she was teaching at the time, and together we headed to the hospital. Sara is my second wife and not the mother of my four children, but she equally shared in my pain.

En route to the hospital, surrounded by afternoon traffic, I heard the news of my son's death from well-wishers calling to offer their condolences. I found myself trapped inside a vehicle with nowhere to run and nowhere to hide from this excruciating pain.

My poor wife could only sit and watch as I agonized over the loss of my child, and neither of us could do anything to expedite the trip to the hospital. The travelers around us in the traffic jam could not understand or share this personal grief that was happening just a few feet from their respective cars.

Ryan had just made the high school football team and had accepted a ride from one of his classmates to go home and pick up his football cleats. On the way home, they stopped by a local gas station. While there, they met another group of friends, and upon leaving, they got into a race with the other friend's car. The car Ryan was in lost control, plunged into a ditch, and hit a culvert. Ryan was propelled through the windshield at seventy miles per hour. Ryan was the only child who lost his life in the crash.

Many thoughts flooded my mind as I stood at the open casket of my son. The well-meaning father of Ryan's best friend stood there beside me and said that if that were his son lying there, they would have to bury him with his son. But as deep as the pain was at that very moment, I knew that wasn't an option for me as I surveyed the room and looked into the grief-stricken eyes of my three remaining children.

With all the questions directed toward God that were tormenting my soul, I remembered a story that I had read. Author John Gunther Sr. chronicled his son John Jr.'s struggle with a fatal disease in the book *Death Be Not Proud*.

John Sr. detailed his own personal pain of watching his son daily wasting away in a hospital bed. The father prayed daily that God would spare his son and grant a cure from this affliction. "O God, show me the way to cure my son," he prayed.

From his bedside, John Jr. heard his father's insistent plea to God. One day, in a compassionate prayer, John Sr. prayed, "God please. My torment is unsustainable. Help my son get through this illness." Upon hearing this prayer, John Jr. looked at his father with love in his eyes and said, "I will soon be all right, Father. It appears that it is you that God is answering in your prayers. It is you that He is helping." You see, before this time John Gunther Sr. had never once prayed.

As I stood at the gravesite of my child, I could almost hear Ryan speaking to me, calming my broken heart. "Dad, if you could only see the beauty that surrounds me right now... I know you're my father and you love me, but if you could only feel the true love of the Father, you wouldn't be sad for me. You wouldn't want me to come back there. If you truly love me, live your life the way you should so you can one day soon join me."

I wasn't raised in the church; however, there had always been something beckoning me toward a relationship with...Someone. No matter what I did, I never realized or felt that supernatural experience I so desperately desired. For fifteen years, I saw my wonderful, Spirit-filled son live a life of trusting God. Ryan had faith that God would do all that He promised. Up until this time, I had never really gotten the message.

"In my Father's house are many mansions: if it were not so, I would have told you" (John 14:2).

I have long understood the intent of this passage, but finding the key to unlock the door of the house had always eluded me. As I looked down upon the deathbed of my son, I realized that my child had gone home to be with his real father in his Father's house. Ryan now held the key.

Slowly, ever so slowly, has been my journey toward finding the key to one of God's many mansions. It's the same as when you teach a child to write. You hold your child's hand while they form the letters; that is, they form the letters because you are forming them. We love and reason because God loves and reasons and holds our hands through our individual journey.

The realization finally came to me that the key to a complete relationship with God always was within me. All I ever had to do was have faith and believe. And I learned this from my son. "It appears that it is you that God is answering in your prayers. It is you that He is helping."

To every man the day is coming when he will wake to find, beyond all hope, that he has attained it; or else that it was within his reach, and he has lost it forever. On our individual journey, we hope that we have done enough to be rewarded with that key on that day. But the question is, what can we really do to reap that reward in this life before we go on to the next? What can each of us do to assure ourselves a place in one of those mansions?

Of course the answer is simply, we can't. There is nothing we can DO, because it has already been done for us. The Bible is laced with the answer. It's always been right there in front of us.

My purpose for writing this book is an attempt to assist my children and grandchildren on their personal journey toward the discovery of "the key." I was never foolish enough to suppose myself qualified as a theologian or teacher of the Bible, nor have I anything to offer the reader beyond the experiences I have encountered in my own journey. I offer a simple collection of stories from the Bible, attempting to put them into modern, everyday events so their meanings would be better understood.

What I have learned is that a little courage helps more than much knowledge, a little human sympathy more than much courage, and the least tincture of the love of God…more than all.

If any real theologian reads these pages, they will very easily see that they are the work of a layman and an amateur. However, I have believed myself to be restating ancient and orthodox doctrines to the best of my untrained ability. In all my writings I have tried to assume nothing as Scripture from the literary writings of men unless it has been researched and documented by the Holy Bible. In doing so, I profess those tenets.

The key is really about attempting to get out of the hole man has gotten himself into. He has tried to set out on his own, to behave as if he belonged to himself. Author C. S. Lewis said of fallen man, "He is not simply an imperfect creature who needs improvement; he is a rebel who must lay down his arms." Laying down his arms, surrendering, saying that you are sorry, earnestly asking for forgiveness, realizing that you have been on the wrong side of the track, and getting ready to start life over again from the ground floor is the only way out of the hole.

If man had not fallen, this would all be simple, wouldn't it? (See Genesis 3:1–24.) Unfortunately, we now need God's help in order to do something that God, in His own nature, never does at all:

To surrender,
  To suffer,
    To submit,
      To die.

Nothing in God's nature corresponds to this humanistic process at all.

But supposing God became man—suppose our human nature, which can suffer and die, was amalgamated with God's nature in one person—then that one person could help us. This person could do it perfectly because He was God. He cannot die except by being a man. This is the sense in which He pays our debt and suffers for us what He Himself need not suffer at all.

And that's the key.

chapter 1

"IN THE BEGINNING GOD..."

GENESIS 1:1

"In the beginning God created the heaven and the earth."

ON CHRISTMAS DAY in 1968, the crew of Apollo 8 was just rounding the last orbit of the moon before their capsule went hurtling back toward the earth. After the horizon of the moon passed, they got a look at their target, and they were astonished at its beauty...taken aback by its majesty.

There it was—a beautiful, blue marble with white swirling clouds, illuminated against a black mat of space by the sunlight. They were almost without words, and when one of them finally spoke, it was not about any Einsteinian theory that had been concocted. No great lyrics or dramatic reading could describe what they felt. When one of them spoke, it was in a soft whisper. It was a whisper that was heard by a billion people down here on Earth.

And he simply read, "In the beginning God created the heaven and the earth. And the earth was without form, and void; and darkness was upon the face of the deep."

In the biblical Creation story, there is the presumption that God created the heavens and the earth out of nothing. This differs from other religions' stories that there was structure then a struggle. Their god creates out of what already exists, merely changing its form.

Not so with the true God. In the Genesis story, there was no struggle...there was no rebuilding. God simply spoke, and with His word came existence. The Bible states that all things are made by Him. There was a time when there were no things...now, all things. "In the beginning was the Word, and the Word was with God, and the Word was God" (John 1:1). The Word, Jesus Christ, was in the beginning with God, and all things were made through Him, and without Him nothing came into being.

Colossians 1:16 reads, "For by Him were all things created, that are in heaven, and that are in earth, visible and invisible." All there is—powers, rulers, authorities...all things—were made by Him and for Him. Revelation 4:11 states, "Thou art worthy, O Lord, to receive glory and honour and power: for thou hast created all things, and for thy pleasure they are and were created."

All things!

There comes a time for all of us when we no longer need to have something continually proven any longer. *We just believe.* We call that faith. It comes in all shapes and sizes and wrappings, and it doesn't always have to do with religion.

I believe there is something really important that needs to be addressed: God created the heavens and the earth, but He did not create them as a finished product. He created them as a continuing process. "The earth was without form, and void; and darkness was upon the face of the deep....And God said, Let there be light" (Gen. 2). Notice there is a formula. There is a pattern here, and I think the pattern is very important for us to understand for our lives.

The Hebrew word for "without form" means "chaotic," and the Hebrew word for "void" simply means "empty." That's the primitive state of existence on this earth, and when your life regresses or relapses to that primitive state, it will go to one of these qualities. Your life will be either chaotic—you can't get hold of anything; it's just going all over the place; it has no form to it—or it will be void, empty.

That is the state of our lives if we are not listening to and acting upon the Word of God. That's our state before the Word of God comes into being in our lives.

In the Creation story, when the Word of God came, in the first three days God began to shape structure out of the formlessness. He did that by dividing the light from the darkness, the heavens from the seas, and sea from the land.

On day four, God began to address the emptiness, and He began to put a corresponding life form, or an inhabitant, into the environment He had just created. Into the sky He put light, the sun and the moon. Then he added the winged creatures. He put all the fish that swim in the sea, and on the land He put plants, insects, and animals to walk the land. And then on day six, He made people to dwell in the environment He had created.

But why? Why did He do all of this? That is the character of God. God always provides for us all that we need before we need it. To God there is no such thing as an unwanted child, and that could certainly refer to you or me.

Not only has He planned for us, but He also provides for us everything we need... and does it to this day.

We need to understand that this is no little accomplishment. It's so easy to go about our everyday lives and take for granted the fact that the sun will be there to give us light and warmth, that the plants will maintain the right amount of oxygen for us to breathe, that there will be enough water for us to drink, and so on. And we may, during that day, remember from where all this came and say under our breath, "Thank You, God. We give you praise for them."

Sometimes we need to stop and remember... remember that this whole set-up is part of a well-orchestrated plan, a complete environment with not one single "uh-oh."

A few years back, some of the brightest people on earth, along with some of the wealthiest, put their respective resources together in an attempt to make a self-contained environment that could sustain life and quite possibly be used in our terrestrial space travels. They called the experiment Biosphere 2. You may remember reading about it.

About thirty miles north of Tucson, Arizona, the biosphere contained approximately 7.2 million cubic feet of space and everything needed to comprise an environment that would be continually self-sustaining to human life. The facility cost in excess of 200 million dollars.

The biosphere was a dome, or a big round tent. They placed inside of it every type of plant that would produce food and oxygen. They also placed the vertebrates and invertebrates that were needed, as well as insects to pollinate the plants. At last, the biosphere was ready to accept the eight people who were to live in this dome for two years. And then the doors closed.

After just one year, nineteen out of the twenty-seven vertebrate animals were dead. All of the pollinating insects were dead, most of the invertebrates were dead, and the people were so hungry they had to smuggle food in through the air vents because the press was watching. Of course, a short time later the eight inhabitants finally surrendered and admitted that they just could no longer survive under those conditions.

Now, if we, as reasonable, thinking people, contrast this fiasco that combined the most brilliant minds known today and enormous wealth with what God has done, I think we can better appreciate the Creation story.

We all know that the blue whale is the largest mammal on the face of the present-day earth. It is so large that the next largest animal, the African elephant, isn't even as large as one of the whale's pectoral fins.

However, the blue whale is nothing compared to some of the natural structures on Earth. If you could physically take one hundred blue whales and place them in a very large jar, it would take approximately a million of these one hundred–count blue whale jars to fill up Mt. Everest.

But, Mt. Everest, in proportion to the face of the earth, is nothing. You could stack one hundred mountains the size of Mt. Everest on top of one another and it wouldn't even make a good whisker upon the face of the earth.

But, the earth is nothing compared to our sun. You could put a million of our earths inside the sun and not fill it up. Of course, our sun is nothing compared to some of the larger stars. You could put over 50 million of our suns into the star Antares, and it wouldn't fill it up.

The star Antares is nothing compared to the size of our galaxy. You could take billions upon billions of stars the size of Antares and not even remotely begin to fill up our galaxy.

But, our galaxy is nothing compared to the size of other galaxies in the universe. There are billions upon billions upon billions of galaxies in our universe.

Now, here's the kicker: the universe is 99.9999 percent EMPTY. When you think of a God who could create this universe in perfect balance, which is still in perfect balance after all these millennia, by just speaking it into existence—and you compare that with the wealthiest and brightest human beings on earth who can't even sustain eight people in a tent for a year—well, you get the picture.

"In the beginning God…"

chapter 2

WE MUST HAVE BOUNDARIES

GENESIS 3:24

"He drove out the man; and he placed at the east of the
garden of Eden Cherubims, and a flaming sword which
turned every way, to keep the way to the tree of life."

MAYBE THE BEST way to get into this Garden of Eden business is to see it as an attempt to describe what went wrong in the first place. That's really what it's all about, isn't it?

God made the world and gave it to His highest creation to look after and bask in, a good world with every detail in place, every need anticipated and provided for: food for the body, beauty for the eye, enough work to do to challenge the sense of accomplishment, and enough recreation including intimate companionship to give it a little spice. It just didn't get any better than that. *What went wrong?*

The world was the product of the Lord God's handiwork, the world that God had made through His word, that He spoke into being, that intricate and magnificent created order that was essentially...good. But now there was a flaw in the script, and it was written in by the blatant disobedience of the very ones for whom the gift of creation was made. What went wrong?

I think the story of the garden is a story about things that were intended to be so right, turning out so wrong. If you attempt to find Eden on the map, it's not there. It doesn't have any coordinates on a Mercator projection.

I think you'll find Eden when you look inside your own heart. When you look inside, you see how true it is. It's a descriptive account of the way we are. It's a picture of human tendency, a snapshot, if you will, of the human soul, a portrait in living color, not of the way we're made, but of the way we *act*.

It's a biography; in fact, it's an autobiography. It's not about yesterday only.

It's about today as well. It's not only about what was. It's about what is right now. And, of course, it's not just about two people.

In the beginning, there was a garden. As the Hebrew people sat in the evenings around the campfire telling the story of Creation, can you imagine the appeal and impact a garden had on a people fresh from the scorching desert? It was God's garden, a lush, pleasant place…a paradise. The Creator placed His highest creation in that idyllic setting and invited him to enjoy. It was his, or theirs, because He made them male and female, different but equal and complementary.

He bestowed on them blessings, responsibility, and the most daring gift a creator can ever bestow, the gift of choice. You are free to choose, even to choose disobedience. That's the pinnacle of creativity, I think. Here are the boundaries…all gardens have boundaries. To be a creature is always to have boundaries. "Every bit of it is yours; it's all yours. Just take care of it." Remember that you are not the Creator. Don't ever think you can be God. That way of thinking can only lead to alienation.

So they began in the garden. And for a while, they did remember. They remembered to whom they belonged, and they were deliriously happy. Genesis 2:25 tells us, "And the man and his wife were both naked and were not…ashamed" (AMP). That's Hebrew talk for original innocence and purity of conscience.

What a portrait of the good life! The godly intended life, the way God designed it to be—for everybody—fulfillment, joy, and intimate companionship unashamedly celebrated between the man and the woman on that level and even higher…between both of them and God.

It's so good that God Himself is pictured coming down in the evening at twilight when the breeze blows, to walk in the garden with His friends. Isn't that an idyllic picture? Isn't that what we would like to do with our Friend? All is harmonious and trusting.

It's how we were made. I think the writers are saying, "That's God's intention. That's the point and goal of creation; intimate fellowship within the species and with Creator." There is a catechism in Westminster that says, "The chief end of man is to glorify God and enjoy Him forever." *Enjoy Him!* That's why we were made—the fulfillment and sheer happiness of garden life.

But, that audacious gift of choice was there. The freedom was real. Freedom is exhilarating, but it can be terribly frightening because it throws responsibility for its consequences right back at YOU. If you're free to choose, you can't blame what goes wrong on somebody else. When God created us, He didn't make puppets/marionettes on a string; He made us with a deeply implanted sense of the moral and independent will that requires making choices.

So, in slithers the snake, the symbol of the temptation to *do* less than the best you know, the temptation to *be* less than the best you can be, the temptation to disobey. If freedom is real, the responsibility of disobedience is real. The snake slithers in, representing the temptation to turn away. He does not represent sin per se. God didn't create sin, but God did create people truly free to choose, and that means free to turn their backs on His benevolent creatorship.

How smooth and oily temptation can be. There is brilliant psychological insight in this writing. First, the serpent sows a hint of uncertainty, a tiny pinch of doubt in the woman's mind. "Did God really say you should not eat of every tree in the garden? Surely He didn't say that, did He? Maybe you misunderstood. He told us, let's see, 'You shall not eat of the fruit of this tree, or you will die.' I heard Him." The snake doesn't debate; the seed of doubt is already planted. Slowly it festers. Uncertainty works best by insinuation, and then, when left alone, it spreads its own infection.

The snake grabs Eve's attention. Next he introduces a denial of any bad consequences of disobedience. "Come now, Eve. You know God wouldn't treat you that way. He's a good God. What possible harm could it do? Besides, let me tell you the dynamics here. Why do you think He imposed a limitation on you? He knows if you just step over the boundary, you'll be like Him. You can decide things. He put the leash on you for His own protection."

When you read these passages of the Bible, it makes sense, doesn't it? Temptation excuses always do. They sound perfectly plausible when you look at them from just one side.

Temptation always has its rationale. So she wavers, just as we all often do, teetering between the "I really shouldn't," and the "why not?" Between what we know we should do and what we know we shouldn't. The serpent waits as the battle rages inside. And it does. Finally, thrown off balance by uncertainty, attracted by the glitter of the exotic, lulled by false assurances, and lured to do "her own thing," the woman makes her choice. She disobeys. Just a little bit, that's all. Why is it such a big deal?

In this short story, we are led directly into the basic nature of sin. The basic nature of sin is not doing dastardly deeds.

It's bigger than that, worse than that, more serious than that.

Doing dastardly deeds is the *result* of sin. Those sins are nothing more than misplaced loyalty. The basic nature of sin is the attempt to usurp God's sole right of sovereignty. The inveterate tendency is to act as if we are God and the world revolves around us.

Adam and Eve were guilty of arrogance, inflated self-importance. They assumed the right to decide where their ultimate allegiance would lie. C. S. Lewis wrote in *Mere Christianity*, "If you are His and you focus on Him, you *can't* choose wrongly." He simply will not let you. In your mind you may be going in the wrong direction, only to find out that is the very way He intended for you to go all along.

Adam and Eve stepped over the boundary of creatureliness in order to try to be God. When you first recognize your vulnerability of being human and not Godlike as the snake had promised, the first thing you realize is your nakedness. Before you weren't ashamed, and now you are. God never once left your side in the garden...you left His. Mark Twain once wrote, "Man is the only animal that blushes—or needs to."[1]

Walter Russell Bowie wrote a powerful line in *The Interpreter's Bible* that I think adequately applies here: "Try to know better than God, to break the *laws of life*, to imagine that our cleverness and our clutching after power can say the final word, and we stand at the end of the day dumb before the quietness of God." I think that's a true picture of what judgment is really about.

Although Adam and Eve forfeited paradise, they were not abandoned by God. "And Lord God made garments of skins for the man and his wife and clothed them" (Gen. 3:21).

I see a pledge of God's refusal to give up on His creation. Here they are stripped of innocence, shorn of fellowship, cut off by their own doing from the fullness of divine relationship. By all rights, it should have been an unmitigated disaster. Yet, God's mercy provided the means by which they could, with dignity, still stand in the holy presence. They sinned, they had been disloyal, they turned their backs, and they *royally blew it*. But in the meantime, God, out of His unfailing grace, took the initiative to bridge the chasm.

The Bible, in its entirety, is a collection of love letters from God to His creation, and the garden is part of the total revelation that culminates in Christ. Thanks to Him, we stand with redeemed humanity before God. Eden is God's original intention, thwarted momentarily by our sinfulness, but it's our ultimate destination. As Eve's lips touched the forbidden fruit, the cross appeared on the horizon.

chapter 3

ON SETTLING DOWN IN HARAN

GENESIS 11:32

"The days of Terah were two hundred and five years: and Terah died in Haran."

"... and Terah died in Haran." Period. That's it. That's all we know about him other than he was the father of Abram. He's a part of the coming together of a nation's story. The city Ur, where Terah and his family lived, was an interesting place, to say the least. It was the focal point of a great moon-worshiping cult...a pagan center.

Maybe the reason they moved was because Terah wanted to take his family out of that environment. Maybe he was included in the "call" from God that came to Abram. Maybe God spoke to the father as well as to the son. We just don't have that information or the background of it. What we do know is that Terah, for some reason, failed to see the journey all the way through. He stopped in Haran.

He had enough faith to start out on the trip, enough faith to make him dissatisfied with paganism. He just didn't go far enough. He just couldn't make himself push on. "I'm going to stay right here where I am." *And that's what he did.* "...and Terah died in Haran."

Maybe what the writer is trying to convey to us is that more people than Terah have settled down in Haran. I don't think this place, Haran, is just simply a matter of longitude or latitude; it's a place in the soul. Maybe a lot of us live there...the midpoint:

Between the flicker of a dream and fulfillment.
Between the first rush of becoming a new Christian and the
excitement of spiritual growth
Between Ur and the Promised Land

We settle in Haran, the place of *not yet*. But we don't have to settle there in Haran. I think that's the point of the story. There's nothing anywhere that says we're required to stay and put down roots in Haran.

Abram followed his dream to the end and became Abraham, the father of a nation, and Terah settled at the halfway house. Author John Oxenham wrote, "You'll never know the wonder, the grandeur, or the glory of the Bible's story of redemption until you see it against the backdrop of the mire in which it begins. You'll never know the miracle of your own salvation until you've looked squarely and honestly at the blackness of your own heart."

Three major religions look back on Abraham with awe, respect, and appreciation. In Islam, Judaism, and Christianity, he is the primary patriarch. He was not perfect; in fact, he lied to save his own skin, he put his wife in terrible jeopardy, and he even argued with God in a brazen fashion.

However, Abraham brought a new beginning, a fresh approach to the dilemma of what to do about the human condition. Before Abraham, the stage was in darkness, the cast was scattered, the original script had been shredded, and there was no plot to the story. In fact, there was not even a theme.

One man emerged for a new storyline and cracked the crust of humanity's shell just wide enough for God to wiggle His finger in. Why Abraham? We call Abraham the father of the faith because somehow he heard, he felt, he sensed the beckoning of God, and he stepped out in pure faith without knowing where his next step would take him. Isn't that the meaning of true faith? Anybody can be faithful when they know what's coming. In Hebrews 11:1 we find faith as "the substance of things hoped for, the evidence of things not seen."

Father Abraham, a man who made himself available to God, didn't settle and die in Haran.

chapter 4

AND THE BEAT GOES ON

GENESIS 12:1–9; HEBREWS 11:8–10
"And I will make of thee a great nation, and I will bless thee…"

CHAPTERS 1 THROUGH 11 of Genesis are not the oldest part of the Bible. They appear first, but they were not written first. People who were a part of the story wrote them in retrospect from the vantage point of a place within the story. They were looking back as if to say, "Here's the stage setting for the drama going on around us."

Noted author G. Ernest Wright wrote that the biblical story is God's story, and that story really gets underway with the calling of a people, taken entirely by surprise, to be His special agents of human rescue.

The story isn't over yet. You and I arrived in the middle of it. Much has happened before our arrival, and there's still more to come. The first eleven chapters of Genesis are the setting for the story, put there to demonstrate why the rescue was necessary. They don't depict the rescue; they depict the problem.

They show the mess humanity got into on its own, through its rebellion, through its cursedness, through its misuse of the freedom granted by God in the beginning, and using the freedom, instead of for God's glory, *for its own glory*. We all commit treason to the love of God.

Almost immediately after the Creation story where everything was
   good, it got bad…
      And then it got worse…
         And then the whole bottom fell out, collapsed, disintegrated,
            and came apart as humankind, left to its own devices, saw its
            misguided ambition tumble into chaos.

The biblical authors were writing a description of what seems to be a predictable human tendency. Noted author G. K. Chesterton wrote, "Life lived without recognition of its dependence on God sooner or later—and usually sooner—comes apart at the seams."

As the stories of the Book of Genesis—creation, the garden, Cain and Abel, the Flood, the Tower of Babel—unfold before us, I dare say that if the writers of these early stories were able to view our world today, they would be saddened, but I don't think they would be surprised. This is what happens apart from God.

So, let me tell you some good news to draw these painful stories of early Genesis together and set us on the road that leads to the rest of the story. *The good news* doesn't negate or deny any of the preceding. *The good news is that there is a rescue party.*

The rescue of the human family from itself, from its own deeply ingrained misuse of its freedom, can be seen on two levels. Maybe another way to say it is that there are two heroes in the rescue story.

The first is that remarkable biblical character Abraham. As I mentioned before, three major religions look back on him with awe, respect, and appreciation. In Islam, Judaism, and Christianity, he's a primary patriarch.

Abraham emerges as the basis for the beginning of a new storyline. Why Abraham? I have no earthly idea. I suspect Abraham himself never fully understood the Lord God's motivation in calling him. That would resonate perfectly with the experience of anybody else who ever received a "call."

What we are talking about here is a man of faith, a man of integrity, a man who recognized his dependence on God and trusted God, even without having all his questions answered. He wasn't perfect, but he's the closest we've seen yet to the garden ideal of living within the boundary and acknowledging the primacy of God.

The second hero is God Himself. As those keepers of the old record lay it out for us, we see the almighty God of the universe surveying the wreckage of human disintegration, grieving over the hurt people have brought upon themselves, wanting to punish injustice yet without destroying personhood, wanting to help and restore without undermining freedom, and determining that the only way to do it consistent with His character is to win people back to Him...one by one.

That's the stage, the setting for the biblical epic, the biblical drama of human redemption, when God, having enough of it *rolls up His sleeves.* He could have waved His magic wand and made it all better. Perhaps He wrestled with that possibility, just as Jesus wrestled with the meaning of His Messiahship in the temptation stories. He chose, instead, the harder way, the more arduous but more thorough way.

We're a part of that story, you and I. In fact, we're the reason for it. We're a part of that long, extended search-and-rescue mission, which began way back there with one receptive man, and extends now, onward through the centuries.

And the good news is that we mean enough to Him for it all to be worthwhile.

chapter 5

"SHALL NOT THE JUDGE OF ALL
THE EARTH DO RIGHT?"

LLOYD C. DOUGLAS, the author of *The Robe*, used to tell a story of a friend he liked to visit on occasion. This old man was a musician turned violin teacher. He had a sort of studio, a little nook set away in a long row of rooms where other music teachers also worked with students.

"I always liked to go see him," said Mr. Douglas. "I enjoyed talking with him. He had a kind of homely wisdom that was refreshing."

One day he dropped by and just by way of greeting said, "Well, what's the good news for today?" The old man put down his violin, picked up a tuning fork suspended by a silk thread, and struck it a sharp blow with a padded mallet. Then he said, "That's the good news for today. That, my friend, is an A. It was an A all day yesterday, it will be an A all day tomorrow, and next week, and for a thousand years from now. There's a piano across the hall that is hopelessly out of tune. But that, my friend, is an A."

The older I get, the more important permanence becomes to me. It may be just old age, slouching now as I am into the springtime of my senility, but I think it's more than that. I seem to have a greater interest and more respect for what *endures*.

Old Captain Ahab had it right. In *Moby Dick*, Herman Melville's masterpiece, Captain Ahab would go down into the bowels of the ship and tighten the carpenter's vise on his hand as tightly as he could stand it, saying, "I like to feel somethin' in this slippery world that won't budge."

The Genesis story of Abram and Sarai takes us all over the place in their respective adventures in the Bible, but the one thing that keeps surfacing out of all the stories is that there is—

One we can point to...
> that won't budge,
> > that's fixed,
> > > that endures with a steady, faithful *abidingness*.

That's one of the great Bible words... *abide*. I looked it up in the King James Version, and it's found approximately eighty-nine times.

"Shall not the Judge of all the earth do right?" It's Abraham speaking, of course, the old patriarch. He'd caught a glimpse of the nature of God and with revelatory insight had seen something there that was eternally consistent and faithful. He wasn't all that sure about people, but he knew that God could be counted on to do what was right and just and good, because, well, it was built in; it was inherent, if you will.

The writer tells that God came down from heaven to talk with Abraham, almost like two old friends. The patriarch at this point is ninety-nine years old. It had been years since he left Ur, ventured into Haran where he departed from his father, Terah, and came to this new land the Lord had promised him. The Promised Land. He'd been young and vigorous then with a lot to learn. And he had learned a lot. He had grown. Now his white hair wafts in the breeze as the two of them stand on the side of the hill under the old oak and look down at the wicked city of Sodom, to the southeast.

They talked awhile, and then God poured out His heart. "The outcry against Sodom is great. Their sin is very grave." (See Genesis 18:20.)

For a moment, Abraham just stood there, and then his face turned white, his hands clenched, his mouth went dry as the impact of it hit him. God is about to destroy Sodom.

"Oh, but not everybody," Abraham cried. "Surely not everybody. You don't really mean that. It doesn't seem fair. What about the people down there who are righteous? Will they be destroyed too, along with the rest? There must be some...50...30...10?" Ol' Abraham tried to cut the best deal he could.

In Marc Connelly's great play, *Ol' Man Adam An' His Chillun*, which was made into the movie, *Green Pastures*, there is a scene where God sends His lieutenant Gabriel down to the earth to investigate the destruction and havoc created by the Flood in the time of Noah. When Gabriel returns to heaven to report on his investigative tour, God asks him how it is, and in a Black, Southern dialect, the archangel says, "Oh, Lawd, it's turrible. It's downright awful. There ain't nothin' fastened down there no more. Everything nailed down is acomin' loose."

Sometimes it seems that way, doesn't it? But I don't believe it's really true. The natural order and the moral order are the same as they've always been. Some things change but haven't come loose. The Ten Commandments, or the Sermon on the Mount, haven't budged an inch. They are still fixed, impregnable, permanent, abiding truths, which, like the everlastingness of God Himself, go on from age to age, eternally the same, and, if we open our eyes and our hearts, we will see this *abidingness* as we travel through this life. *He is always an "A."*

As Abraham continued to bargain, he kept edging closer and closer to the divine heart until finally he realized something that all of us need to be sure of...can be certain of: Whatever else we may want to say about God, He has to be at least as good as we are. If He made us, if He is *the* Creator, then He must at least be as good as His own creation.

The truth of it dawned on Abraham out there under the old oak. There is an inherent rightness in the character of God that just keeps coming out over and over again, a built-in goodness that's deeper and more genuine than anything we can ever imagine.

When Abraham realized it, he rested his case by making a final appeal to God's own nature:

"Shall not the Judge of all the earth do right?"

I know it's an old story, but being old doesn't make it obsolete. The eternal God of the universe, the judge of all the earth, can never be false to Himself. He can never be untrue to His own character.

Ol' Abraham discovered God's faithfulness, His *abiding* love on the side of a rocky, barren hill in the Middle East, out under an oak tree. "Shall not the Judge of all the earth do right?" There are many questions Abraham couldn't answer...so much he couldn't understand, just like us.

Hurdles fell in front of Abraham, and roadblocks took him out of his way just as they do to us today. But I have an idea Abraham somehow would affirm what we're going through. And maybe all of us, in our better moments, have a kind of instinctive faith that, however much there is in the divine nature, we can't fathom. However much there is that's beyond us, there's a rightness, a justice, a basic goodness, a personal caring that outshines our own.

The Bible calls that the abiding faithfulness of God. Ol' Abraham counted on it…depended on it…and I think we can follow his lead with utmost confidence in a true gentleman and His Word.

That, my friend, is an A. It was an A all day yesterday, it will be an A all day tomorrow, and next week, and for a thousand years from now.

chapter 6

STUCK IN THE MIDDLE WITH YOU

GENESIS 26:17–33

"And Isaac digged again the wells of water, which they
had digged in the days of Abraham his father."

THE MOTHER OF President Dwight David Eisenhower was interviewed a
short time before her death. The reporter asked, "Mrs. Eisenhower, I know
you must be very proud of your son." Her eyes sparkled, and she said tartly, "I
certainly am, young man. Which one of my sons are you talking about?" She
had four sons, and she was proud of them all.

"Alas, poor Yorick," err, I mean Isaac, the son of a great man, and the father
of a great man. There he was, caught in the middle, a non-entity between two
bright entities, an ordinary stone between two diamonds, a Pigpen between a
Linus and a Lucy.

The son of Abraham and the father of Jacob...Jacob. Wow! The kid turned
out to be a whizbang, a ball of fire, a veritable cauldron of seething energy, and
in time, a pillar of faith, the progenitor of the twelve tribes of Israel. Israel, in
fact, became his new name. He was the most complex, multifaceted, and just
plain interesting character of all the figures in the Old Testament...and Isaac
was his father.

Poor old Isaac! Put him up against either his father or his son, and the
contrast immediately is glaring. The God of our fathers, as the Hebrews would
later say, the God of Abraham, Isaac, and Jacob. The only reason they would
even include Isaac in the formula is just because he was there—

the link,
the one who joined together the two,
the bond between the generations.

Take him out of context, and what is there outstanding to commend him? How many parent/child duos in history come to mind right off the bat?

- Pitt the elder and Pitt the younger in England
- John Adams and John Quincy Adams
- George H.W. Bush and George W. Bush

You really can't think of many. The obverse is more common. It's not easy to be the offspring of celebrity status in any setting. Notoriety may open doors, but it puts the squeeze on a child in a way not many can wriggle free from. And when your relative greatness comes from both sides, you're really boxed in.

Isaac was no creator. He was no formulator of new ideas, new programs, new religious advances.

He was not an innovator. That distinction belonged to his father, Abraham. Abraham, who was all things, cutting a wide swath in history, leaving the human situation different from what it had been before.

Even geographically the contrast was striking. Abraham began way over in Ur of the Chaldeans, moved up to Syria, then down into the land of Canaan, once even dipping down into Egypt, where he tried to pawn off his wife Sarah as his sister to save his hide.

Isaac, on the other hand, *never moved out of his little circle of friends in Palestine.*

Maybe we need to give him a little credit, cut him a little slack. He preserved and kept alive the faith and values of his more illustrious father.

Maybe he didn't create, but he conserved...

Maybe he didn't build, but he maintained...

Maybe he didn't originate, but he tended and preserved intact.

Elmer Clark, the great Methodist historian, has told a story many times that comes out of the mountains of east Tennessee. Back in the 1930s when dams were being built in that beautiful mountain range area to stop erosion and renourish the land, there lived on a small plot of land an old farmer whose house was about to be claimed by the rising waters.

Eminent domain was alive and well even then. The government had built him a new house...a better house on higher ground, and they told him it was his...*free.* But the old man refused to leave his cabin.

Finally the Tennessee Valley Authority (TAV) engineer, who himself was from that region and knew something about the fears and stubbornness of mountain people, went to talk with the old-timer. He quickly realized that the man's reluctance to move had to do not so much with the house itself but with the fire that was burning in the fireplace.

"My grandfather built that fire a hundred years ago, and he never let it go out. There weren't any matches in those days, and there weren't any neighbors to borrow fire from. He built it originally with flint and steel. He kept it alive, year after year, winter and summer. When he died, my father tended it. When my father died, I tended it, and none of us ever let it go out. *I ain't about to move off and leave the fire my grandfather built."*

The engineer, with compassion and maybe a touch of genius, left and came back later with some more men and a huge kettle. Gently they gathered up the glowing coals in the old man's fireplace, carried them up the hill to the new house, and poured them out on the hearth and kindled them up again.

It's Important Not to Let the Fire Go Out!

Change the symbol from fire to water, and you have the story of Isaac. He dug again the wells, the record says, that his father, Abraham, had dug years before. The wells the Philistines had clogged during the interim. (See Genesis 26:15.) He dug them out again until they were flowing with fresh, pure water once more.

Isaac himself may not have been all that creative in matters of the spirit, but he had an instinctive recognition of what constituted his father's greatness, and he had a reverence for it. He not only saw the bigness of Abraham's faith, but he also knew that's what he wanted for himself, and he dug until fresh water came bubbling up for him.

Every time I read this story, I wonder why it's put in the Bible if old Isaac was such a bland individual.

Hamburger where his father was filet mignon...

a flickering, dimly burning candle where his father was neon lights.

As I read and reread this story, I can't help but wonder if it's not showing a little, or a whole lot, about people...well...many of us. Maybe the Abrahams of the world bring new vitality into the world, but it's the Isaacs who keep it fresh and transmit it.

Maybe we all are redigging wells in our Father's world. Maybe the story reflects a little of us who are trying to emulate and live up to what our Father would have us do.

I try to remember that. After all, there's no new gospel. There's no new novel truth about God and God's relationship to His people, to sin, to the world.

I think we're here "to keep the fire going," as the old farmer did, to redig wells as Isaac did, and to try to find fresh ways to proclaim *abiding* truth. Maybe certain times plead for an Abraham. Maybe we need the creative,

the daring,
the pulsating,
the dramatic.

But there's also a role for the quieter virtues, the holding on steadfastly to what has, through the years, proven helpful and uplifting and good. The world couldn't surge forward without its Abrahams, but it would be a far less pleasant place to live without its Isaacs.

I don't think God asked Isaac to be an Abraham or a Jacob, but he did ask him to be an Isaac. He didn't ask him to be great, but He did ask him to be responsive.

And the big thing about Isaac is that he was where he was, and maybe after all…that is truly what greatness is all about.

chapter 7

SOME GET THE ELEVATOR, SOME THE SHAFT

GENESIS 29:25

"In the morning, behold, it was Leah."

AFTER ALL HE'D been expecting. After all he'd anticipated. After psyching himself up for Rachel, Leah is what he got. It's a funny story in a way. Can't you just picture the boys telling it over and over down at the Cracker Barrel, roaring with hysterics, slapping their knee about how ol' Laban had bested that young whippersnapper Jacob.

Talk about dirty tricks.

Talk about conniving duplicity.

Talk about unspeakable disappointment…there it is, all wrapped up in one little sentence: "In the morning, behold, it was Leah." *Leah!*

We need to be honest; this is basically a chauvinistic story. This is a guy thing. Much of the Old Testament, especially the early Old Testament, is written with male assumptions pretty well in place.

Here's our cast of characters: Jacob, the protagonist; Laban, the father-in-law; and his two daughters, Leah and Rachel. And the storyline was simple: Jacob could work for his future father-in-law for seven years, and the lovely Rachel was his. *Right!*

I don't know when Jacob realized he'd been had. I have no idea when it dawned on him what Laban had done to him. The Bible is very interesting that way; it's unmistakably explicit yet remarkably discreet. The Bible doesn't tell us how it happened but leaves us in no doubt about *what* happened. That single, poignant sentence, "In the morning, behold, it was Leah."

Not Rachel, not his beloved, not the apple of anticipation, not the sweetheart of Sigma Chi, but that other one, her older sister, weak-eyed Leah.

How could it have turned out this way? The morning sun breaking in through the tent flap revealed the full measure of his blighted hopes. "In the morning, behold, it was Leah."

> She wasn't what he really wanted,
>   she wasn't what he had dreamed of,
>   she wasn't what he had worked for and looked forward to.
>   She was a pale, poor substitute for what he'd been
>   anticipating.

The reality came leagues below the promise of the vision. And the Bible says it so simply, and with such an economy of words. "In the morning, behold, it was Leah." *The ultimate disappointment of realized expectations!*

It's a great story, this old, primitive tale from another era and halfway around the world. Even today, some anticipation, when realized, is not worth it. Is this old story nothing but another one of those found in the Bible to tell us of another story...one not so out of date even today? Is Leah only a person who lived once upon a time, or could she also represent a whole raft of disappointments in our own day that also don't live up to anticipated billing?

I think if we look close enough, we can see the face of Leah reflected in our inordinate obsession with "things." What other people in history have had what we have in the way of personal possessions...things?

When has there been a time when people, at least people like us, had more? And yet, *when has there been a time when more of us have felt emptier?* Leah all over again.

- We can gather, but it doesn't seem to satisfy.
- We can accumulate, but it doesn't seem to comfort.
- We have it all, and yet the center is missing.

It occurred to me recently, upon hearing the news of the deaths of Paul Newman, Michael Jackson, Farah Fawcett, Paul Harvey, Walter Cronkite, and many other notable people, that the intensive care unit in a hospital is probably the most democratic place I know. More raw equality there, I guess, than in church, school, or town meetings. In the ICU, color, race, influence, and money don't really make much difference. One realizes then just how transient, how ephemeral, physical things are.

These are all too often hard lessons. Lessons that are as old as the biblical patriarchs and yet as modern as this morning's newspaper. "In the morning, behold, it was Leah."

T.S. Eliot wrote in 1925, "We are the hollow men, gorging ourselves with the insubstantial and waking up empty."

I don't think I would be too far off if I were to summarize the story this way: As long as Leah is in the tent, living will be a drag. You can't be whole, you can't be healthy, you can't be complete as a Christian while a part of you is not acknowledging God's sovereignty. Confess the Lord as Lord for you...and watch Leah turn into Rachel. I think that is essentially how the Bible story ends.

Jacob was disappointed, Jacob felt cheated, and Jacob was frustrated. What he thought he was getting turned out to be a fraud. Many since can understand that. But he went back...he turned it around. And if I may be so bold... "In the morning, behold the *joy*, it was Rachel."

chapter 8

THE MATURING OF A REAL STINKER

GENESIS 45:1–11, AMP

"And Joseph said to his brothers, Come near to me, I pray you.
I am Joseph your brother, whom you sold into Egypt."

TALK ABOUT A chance to get even...talk about an opportunity to enjoy sweet revenge.

He had 'em in his hand.
He had 'em by the throat; why,
He had 'em ever which way but loose.

What goes around comes around, they say, and it had come around here, almost a perfect symmetry. The very people who had been ugly to him in the early days of his life were now completely at his disposal. The verses in the forty-fifth chapter of Genesis are the climax of one of the longest and most fully developed stories in the Old Testament.

The Joseph saga is a story written on more than one level. It's the account of a changed, matured man, and it's a testimony to the guiding, directing hand of God through the twists and turns of the human pilgrimage. But, I'm jumping ahead; let's go back to the beginning.

The young man Joseph was a brat. That's the prelude; that's the starting line. He had all those brothers, older brothers; he was the baby of the family. The others were the children of Leah. Leah was the mother of the older boys, and then along came little Joseph by Rachel. There was clear favoritism shown; unfortunately, blatant favoritism. Both parents doted on the boy while the older half brothers seethed. I suspect Leah did, too.

I know it didn't help when Joseph's father bought his favorite a pink polka-dot sports coat with shiny gold buttons and an embroidered, HU (Hebrew University) patch on the pocket.

The seeds of mutiny were planted.

Now the brothers, although not the brightest bulbs in the package, knew this coat wasn't for keeping Joseph warm while tending the sheep at night. So, like any good biblical story up to this time, the brothers plotted to do away with the boy.

They would have killed him—nearly did—if the oldest brother, Judah, hadn't remonstrated with the others, maybe out of a twinge of conscience. Instead, they sold him as a slave to a passing caravan of Midianite traders, who took him down to the land of Egypt. And the biblical cover-ups continue.

For Joseph, it was the first thing in his life he couldn't control. The full-grown, flourishing tree of maturity sometimes starts out of a tiny crack like this, emerging slowly from the tiny seeds of self-doubt. The full impact of Joseph's finiteness slammed him in the face on that caravan ride down to Egypt.

Mercenary slave traders aren't as susceptible to manipulation as doting parents. They simply didn't care about his dreams or his pedigree. They sold him to a wealthy man in Egypt, pocketed the cash, and left; business transaction ended and done.

Harsh as it was and emotionally wrenching, maybe precisely because of that, it marked the beginning of a new-and-improved Joseph. Credit him at least with not allowing his misfortune to cripple him. He couldn't control his fate, but he could control his attitude with which he would face it.

Now he needed all the help he could get because there was a lot more to come. There was that nasty incident involving Potiphar's wife, his owner's spouse, who took an amorous liking to the young stud. She made an offer he, well, refused.

It, of course, cost him plenty because she turned on him when he turned her down, and the next thing you know he was thrown into prison.

From prince and heir apparent, to a wealthy ranch owner in his own land, to a prison inmate in a foreign country without influence, without resources, without even Johnny Cochran as a public defender to say a good word for him…

What kept him going? Where do you turn when there's nowhere to turn? Maybe it's memories, or hopes, or someone, or something…back there or out there.

There is a story about a lady by the name of Gerta Weissman and her reflection on her experience as a prisoner in a Nazi concentration camp in World War II. She survived one of the fortunate ones and later said that when people ask her, "Why did you go on? How did you make it? She confides that there is only one picture that comes to mind. "That moment was when I stood in the first camp I was in and asked myself the most important question of my life. If one wish could be granted to me, what would it be? And then, with crystal clarity, the picture came to my mind. I saw a picture of my father smoking his pipe, my mother working on her needlepoint, and my brother and I were doing our homework. And I remember thinking, my God, it was just a boring evening at home. I had known countless evenings like that. I knew that this simple picture could be, if I held it, the driving force to my survival."

Maybe Joseph held on to something similar, some tie through the gift of memory:

> from his past,
>> from his home,
>>> from his roots,
>>>> from the values of his religious heritage, even if many of
>>>> them hadn't sunk in very deeply before.

He got himself into a lot more trouble but helped others along the way. I think in Joseph's case, surrender and cooperation with God was followed by public recognition. He realized that God was running the show...that he, Joseph, wasn't the ultimate scenario shaper, or decision maker...that he was simply a player, one of many, in a great divine drama.

There's a lot more to this story with Joseph's brothers being forgiven and accepted, but I think the bigger picture of this story is that God doesn't necessarily give special worldly rewards to those who give themselves to Him, but He does give something special, something enormously big. He gives the capacity to bury old grudges, to eliminate the wounds and the hurts of the past, clearing the way for divine reconciliation.

The brothers? Here they come, with hat in hand, no bargaining chips, no leverage. They've come as beggars, and their only hope rests in the magnanimity of the grand Egyptian viceroy. Talk about a chance to get even...he had 'em in his hand. Do you think they would have even bothered to come if they had known? Better to die of simple starvation than humiliation *and* starvation.

Here is drama of the highest order. "I am your brother Joseph, whom you sold into Egypt."

As the brothers stood before the one they had wronged, their sins stared them squarely in their face. The beauty, the wonder, the miracle, the good news...*the gospel* of this story is that there is One greater than Joseph, who wants more than we can ever know, to show forgiveness and blessings to us, with our sins staring us squarely in the face before the One we have wronged.

chapter 9

STOPPING BY ELIM—PART I

EXODUS 15:27, AMP

"And they came to Elim, where there were twelve springs of water
and seventy palm trees; and they encamped there by the waters."

IT'S JUST A simple verse in a long narrative. Like most passages in the Bible,
you really have to stop and think about what you just read. In this particular
passage there is action:

Action before and action after...
lots of action in the middle.
This line represents simply an interlude,
a brief respite,
a chance to catch your breath before you plunge into the
next exciting scene.

But can you read it with imagination? Can you picture the lift it must have
given those dog-tired pilgrims as they plodded across that desert? "And they
came to Elim, where there were twelve springs of water and seventy palm trees;
and they encamped there by the waters."

The Bible stories come out of an area of the world that is harsh, dry, and
unbelievably desolate. It really is difficult to think of any place on earth less
hospitable to the maintenance of human life than that corner of our planet
where three continents come together, the place we call the Middle East. Much
of it is so arid as to be virtually uninhabitable.

The stark severity of the desert influences your whole outlook. I don't
suppose it's an accident that philosophy with its endless theories and specula-
tions came out of the plush, verdant Aegean Islands, but religion came out of
the desert.

Judaism, Christianity, Islam—three of the world's mightiest spiritual forces—are all cradled there in the parched sands of Arabia, the place we're talking about. And why should it be surprising?

When it takes every ounce of effort and energy you possess just to stay alive, you don't have time for speculation and flights of fancy. You think about basic things like:

survival,
   life,
      destiny.

Someone has said, "The desert makes monotheists" (the doctrine or belief that there is only one God), and that pretty well tells it. When you live there, you have to have something bigger than you are to cling to.

Well, that's the panoramic setting for this slender verse from Exodus. The immediate setting is a long, bone-wearying walk out of Egypt. Out of the exuberance of the upcoming Red Sea crossing, the exultation of the victory over Pharaoh had subsided, the harsh reality of journeying set in.

As was with most families, when we set out on a road trip, we would scarcely get out of the driveway before one, and usually all four children, would pipe up from the backseat, "How much farther is it, Daddy? When are we going to get there?"

Well, that's the story ol' Moses had while wandering in the wilderness—and the word *wilderness*, by the way, was an inadequate translation. Whenever you read wilderness in the Bible, substitute *desert* and you'll be closer. See bleak, barren, treeless landscape, from horizon to horizon, and you'll have a more accurate picture but that's the story of their eventual forty year trek. "How much farther is it, Moses? When are we going to get there?"

No sooner were they out of the driveway than the grumbling set in. Exodus calls it "murmuring." That's a great Bible word: murmur, murmur, murmur.

"What has he brought us to? Moses I never did completely trust the guy. What do we really know about his background? Making bricks, after all, wasn't so bad. At least there was something to eat and a little bit of shade to rest in during coffee break. This is progress? We're worse off than before. Have you brought us out here to die, Moses?" Murmur, murmur.

Some wanted to turn on their heels and go back. They very nearly persuaded the rest. But Moses somehow held them together. And on they trudged, maybe not resolutely, but at least continually, mile after mile, day after day, through gritty sand that got into everything they owned.

The wind peppered their faces like bird shot, the sun that beat down mercilessly on their necks, sweat popped, their limbs ached, and thirst, terrible, relentless thirst turned their mouths into cotton.

Despite all of it, they kept going. This was the desert.

And then when it seemed they couldn't take another step, they came to Elim, where there were twelve springs of water and seventy palm trees; and they encamped there by the water.

After all they'd been through, it must have seemed like heaven itself. Call it scrawny, if you like, compared to Waikiki, or Daytona Beach, maybe so, but to them in that setting, it must have looked like *paradise*. An oasis in the desert, a place to rest, to catch up, to clean up, to drink till you popped.

Somebody was even impressed enough to count specifically the number of trees. It's part of the record—the first environmental "green" survey in recorded history. There weren't "several," or a "few," or a "bunch."

There were seventy exactly, each in its place a marvelous and special gift. For the first time in weeks, people talked about grace and blessings and bounty, and, oh, let's not forget about the goodness of God. At least for a moment, a precious interlude between grind and uncertainty, all was right with the world.

Exodus lays it out for us in the simple wording of this text, all we need to make the scene leap to life: "And they came to Elim, where there were twelve springs of water and seventy palm trees; and they encamped there by the waters."

Now, here in the story, as I believe is true in most of the Bible, there is more than just history. While I believe with all my heart each and every word that is printed in the Bible is just as it is written, I also believe there is much, much more depth than what lies at the surface.

May I propose Elim as a symbol, a metaphor, if you will, for all those special points of refreshment and renewal in life that God gives us in our journey, out of bondage, and on to the promise?

First and most obviously—in fact, I guess I've already suggested it—Elim is more than a place. Elim, figuratively, can be any uplifting, reinvigorating experience that brings us respite as we travel and reminds us afresh of our dependence on God.

It doesn't have to be a physical, geographical Elim, and your Elim may not be another's Elim, but from time to time, every person needs to take time off to recoup his physical and spiritual energy.

Author Wayne Muller wrote a book titled *Sabbath*. The entire book is based on finding rest, renewal, and delight in our busy lives. Rachel Naomi Remen, MD, writes of *Sabbath*, "This is a book that may save your life. *Sabbath* offers a surprising direction for healing to anyone who has ever glimpsed emptiness at the heart of a busy and productive life." To perform at your best, you have to do it.

I can identify with a quote from Julia Ward Howe, the nineteenth century social reformer who is best remembered as the author of "The Battle Hymn of the Republic." Once, when she was worn out, weighed down by the cares of the world around her and the load she was carrying, she slumped in her chair and said she was, "Tired...tired way into the future."

The journey across the sands, the giving, the doing, the going, constantly saps us after a while and we simply need a break.

One of my favorite stories about Jesus is the story Mark records when Jesus is at work teaching and healing the people. They flood in for help all day long, even into the night. Finally, He closes the door, withdraws, and goes to Elim for renewal. You see, Jesus knew that no one can be the hand that gives *to* life until it is first the hand that receives *from* life. When things and conditions became too crowded, He went to Elim so that He was able to come back refreshed, ready to give His best.

Elim may take a number of forms: reading, a sudsy bath, a walk in the woods. Friendship can be an Elim, and on and on. You may not believe this, but Sara, my wife, goes to the Elim Beauty Salon and comes back ravishingly refreshed.

Prayer, of course, is Elim. There are springs of water there that never run dry. I believe this "rule" of the refreshment of Elim is there not because somebody thought it ought to be there, but because of the need implanted in our hearts. If you miss it, you feel it, and then, even more tragically, after a while, you don't feel it.

"Twelve springs of water and seventy palm trees." More than you need to renew your strength. Elim is more than a place.

chapter 10

STOPPING BY ELIM—PART II

EXODUS 15:27, AMP

"And they came to Elim, where there were twelve springs of water and seventy palm trees; and they encamped there by the waters."

CHARLES LUTWIDGE DODGSON, a mathematician who taught at Cambridge University in England in the nineteen century, wrote a ponderous math book titled *Euclid and His Modern Rivals*. It is a comprehensive, thick book, his *magnum opus*, that few people read today and few people remember. He stopped at his Elim, the home of a friend, Henry George Lidell, and began telling stories to his friend's young daughters. They were stories of a little girl about their age who fell down through a rabbit hole, into a strange, upside-down world, where a March Hare, a Cheshire cat, and a cantankerous Queen of Hearts lived.

Those wonderful stories, in time, of course, were published under his pen name, Lewis Carroll, and have been loved by generations of children and adults ever since as *The Adventures of Alice in Wonderland*.

It wasn't the planned, intended goal. It was the stopping-off place that made Charles Dodgson and his work treasured by millions. You never know.

Sometimes,
it's the little side steps along the way,
the serendipity,
the Elims that give life its spice and flavor.

Elizabeth Barrett Browning wrote, "Earth's crammed with heaven and every common bush afire with God, but only those who see, take off their shoes." Then she added sardonically, "The rest sit around and pick blackberries."

Now, I personally think blackberry picking itself may be an Elim, but the

41

point is…be ready. Look for the burning bushes God sets ablaze in our paths. Pause long enough to drink from the *spring and rest for a moment in the shade of the palms.*

The text implies, "They came to Elim, where there were twelve springs of water and seventy palm trees; and they encamped there by the waters." *Encamped*, it says.

Not settled, not homesteaded, not put down roots and have the local concrete supplier back up their cement trucks to pour a foundation. They encamped, implying that after the renewal and refreshment, they would vacate the area, put all their garbage into ziplock bags, and place them into the supplied receptacles around the seventy palms.

A parallel and opposite danger of not stopping at Elim at all is the danger of trying to stay there too long, the danger of lingering when God is ready for us to go to move out.

We need the respite, the time out. We need the vacation, the refreshment, the Elim, but a lifetime of Elim is a cop-out, and I just don't see God allowing us to get away with it.

We've seen Jonah try it. He thought Elim was in Spain. God called him to get up and go to Nineveh, and he headed straight in the opposite direction. He ran from his responsibility, as hard as his little legs could run, or sailed as fast he could sail. God had to chase him down, but He did; He used a big fish to do it and brought him back to his assignment.

The disciples thought the Mount of Transfiguration was Elim. "Let's just stay here, Lord, and drink from this water forever. It's wonderful, a mountain-top high. We'll build a church for You. We'll build a church for Moses. We'll build a church for Elijah. We'll start a building fund. We'll buy a new bus and get a brand-new organ."

Dr. Thomas Price Jr., has always said that the two most characteristic words of the New Testament are the little words *come* and *go.*

In the Gospels, they alternate back and forth. Jesus said, "Come…, come and see…, come, ye beloved of My Father…, come unto me, all ye that labor and are heavy laden and I will give you rest."

Come to Elim and be refreshed.

However, He never lets us stay there. He never lets us be content with just what's in it for us. After the *come*, there's always that other word, that divinely imperious word, *go.*

Go and tell what you've seen. Go and sin no more. Go ye into all the world and preach the gospel to every living creature.

Elim is for rest, but not for retirement. Worship is drill practice so you can march into battle. Bible study is for laundering our towel so we can go out and wipe the feet of the dirty and diseased. But God never said we had to do it by ourselves. He tells that He's already done it. He's already done it for us.

It's a long way from Egypt to Canaan, from bondage to freedom, from slavery to maturity.

The Hebrews weren't the only ones who had to cross those sands. It's not an easy journey. Along the way we'll encounter:

dry spells,
  heat,
    abrasiveness,
      thirst,
        fatigue.

There'll be times when we'll want to turn around and go back. Maybe, just maybe, it wasn't all that bad back there. There'll be times when we'll want to give up. There'll be times when the sheer weight of the load will be almost too heavy to bear.

But from time to time, often when you least expect it, you'll come over a rise in the hill, and there stretched out before you will be an oasis just waiting for *you*.

To receive and be blessed, to wash your tired feet, to give you to drink and quench your thirst, and to invite you to rest in the shade before you go your way.

When you stop and think about it, what more could you want for your journey?

"Then they came to Elim, where there were twelve springs of water and seventy palm tree;, and they encamped there by the waters."

chapter 11

OH, YES WE CAN

NUMBERS 13:1–33; 14:1–11, AMP
"If the Lord delights in us, then He will bring us into this land
and give it to us, a land flowing with milk and honey."

DOES ANYBODY READ the Book of Numbers anymore? Maybe Rabbinic students do, or maybe a smattering of scholars of the Torah...and for a couple of weeks every fall, my students of Disciple Bible Study, a thirty-two-week study covering about 85 percent of the Bible.

Noted author Irving L. Jensen wrote of the Book of Numbers, "The Hebrew title of this book is interpreted *In the Wilderness* (*Bemidbar*). It should not be thought of as merely, 'Hebrew History.' All of the things that are written are for our spiritual growth. We learn from the mistakes of the children of Israel so as not to repeat them. Consequently, Numbers is a very important book."

Admittedly, there are a lot of genealogical tables in the Book of Numbers and lists of the make-up of the tribes of Israel. The duties of the priests are predescribed and a *very* careful spelling out of how you should make your offerings to the Lord. If you're big on studying the legal announcements in the newspaper, you'll get a real bang out of reading the Book of Numbers.

The people of God were poised at a critical juncture in their history...God had just brought them out of Egypt...Moses was at the head of the column, but God was the deliverer.

He rescued them from the tyranny of Pharaoh,
    emancipated them from slavery,
        cut a side deal with them on the holy mountain,
        gave them Ten Commandments,
            molded them into a community with a structure they never
            had,

45

> gave them a hope, a dream, and
> promised them that just out there lay this land flowing
> with milk and honey.

All the turmoil they had been through was about to end. At last! They were on the very brink of realizing the triumph for which they had been chosen.

In preparation for the conquest, good ol' Moses sent out twelve spies, one from each of the twelve tribes of Israel, to scout out the land. Probably took a court stenographer to make notes of the topography, the water supply, favorable routes, things to watch for, things to stay away from.

"Bring us back a report," Moses said. "See what the land is like; see whether the people who live in it are strong or weak, whether the land is rich or poor...and, oh yes, bring back some samples of the fruit that's growing there." That's exactly what I would have asked them to do while spying in an unchartered, possibly hostile land...check out the Chiquita bananas and make sure the pomegranates are fresh.

Anyway, off they marched out into the cruel Arabian desert, up into what is now the hill country of southern Israel, to the region around Hebron. Anybody who called it lush would almost have had to be one. But, to the men who had just left the scorching desert sands, it must have seemed a veritable jungle of vegetation.

Figs were growing in plentiful abundance; pomegranates were, well, pomegranating. Now, at this point, you have to wonder about the accuracy of the report of the grapes. I've never been to the grape-producing area of California, but I think the governor of that state would have to bow down to the report coming in from the spies Moses had sent in about the size of the grapes.

The grapes were so large that it took two men to carry a single cluster of them. If you want to see what that looks like, there is a life-sized, to scale, bronze statue of these two spies carrying this bundle of grapes, on steroids, in the front of First Baptist Church, Orlando, Florida. Brother Jim Henry, pastor at First Church, loved this passage in the Bible that much. Either those were some powerful grapes, or a steady diet of manna had swelled the tendency of the Hebrews to exaggerate.

The spies saw this contrast, this panorama laid out before them, and they trembled with excitement. "All this can be ours." But at the same time, here was the dark side, the negative, the problems that stood between them and the realization of the dream. The residents of this land weren't just going to roll over and die.

"Did you see the size of those people? We looked like grasshoppers alongside them."

Back at the camp, the crowd welcomed them and assembled to hear the report. "It's all we've been told...and even more. Look at these samples of the fruit we brought back." The Bible doesn't say there was oohing and ahhing at that point, but there must have been some of that going on. But then, they had to hear the downside.

They couldn't forget about how puny they seemed in contrast to the giants who were the present occupants, so they voted *no*. "We ain't agoin' back. Uh, uh, no way, Jack." You will have to admit, the report was pretty grim. It was a pragmatic, common-sense approach. If at first you don't succeed, don't make a fool out of yourself.

But wait! All was not lost! We had not heard from all the twelve tribes' scouts. There's Caleb, one of the lesser known of the Old Testament characters. Doesn't it often seem that way in the Bible stories? Out of the twelve tribes, only Caleb and Joshua felt any sense of confidence about the prospect. There is no record of the speech that Caleb made at that meeting, but we can probably imagine what was going through his mind. "But, did you see the size of those grapes? And those pomegranates...my, my, my."

After *all* they had just been through, God had taken care of the Egyptians, and the Amalekites, and the hunger and thirst of the people in the desert, how were a few giants around Hebron going to stop them? He promised the land to them. What more do you need? "Let us go at once...for we are well able to overcome it."

How sad that they wouldn't listen to him. The majority report prevailed. Caleb and Joshua lost:

Giants - 10, Pomegranates - 2.

Caleb and Joshua had to be disappointed. Moses was disappointed...and God? Well, God was mad.

God pulled the plug on the whole trip. He halted the pilgrimage and postponed the conquest for a full generation. Of all those who left Egypt, and they numbered in the hundreds of thousands, only two...Caleb and Joshua...made it all the way through the forty years and into the Promised Land.

When all the negatives come at us in the world and they're right outside our very door, maybe we should be more like Caleb and Joshua and dwell on the possibilities, dwell on the positive that has been done in our lives and can be done in our lives, and most importantly, dwell on the faithfulness of God. Let's dwell on the pomegranates that have been promised.

Caleb knew all the problems but was ready to go anyway. I guess the question at this point is…are *we* ready to go?

"Let us go up at once, for we are well able to overcome it."

chapter 12

FAMILY, FAITH, AND FUTURE

DEUTERONOMY 6:1-9

"Hear, O Israel: The Lord our God is one Lord: and thou shalt love the Lord your God with all thine heart, and with all thy soul, and with all thy might."

BISHOP WOODY HEARN told a story about a little boy in New Jersey. He lived in a home with an abusive stepfather, except you can't really call that a home, and you can't really call that living. He existed in a hell house with an abusive stepfather. That's a more accurate way to say it.

One day this little nine-year-old boy was walking down the street near the house when a dog savagely bit him on the arm. Somebody took him to the Baptist hospital there in New Jersey where a number of stitches were given him along with more love, care, and attention than he had ever received in his life.

Later, he was released and returned to his official residence. Bishop Hearn concluded, "While the stitches were still in his arm he left the house and started looking for that dog again."

Some people right next to us have been looking for that dog for quite a while...some of us for a very long time. There is more pain, more violence in diverse forms, and more hurt in our homes than any nation has a right to experience. And, more often than not, the one inflicting the pain isn't even aware of it.

In the New and the Old Testaments, in both Jewish and Christian traditions, the home is considered the fount of spiritual nurture. Religious instruction begins in the home and is the springboard for religious outreach and service.

"Hear, O Israel: The LORD our God is one LORD: And thou shalt love the LORD thy God with all thine heart, and with all thy soul, and with all thy might. And these words, which I command thee this day, shall be in thine heart: And thou shalt teach them diligently unto thy children, and shalt talk of them when thou sittest in thine house, and when thou walkest by the way, and when thou liest down, and when thou risest up. And thou shalt bind them for a sign upon thine hand, and they shall be as frontlets between thine eyes. And thou shalt write them upon the posts of thy house, and on thy gates" (Deut. 6:4–9).

This is from the Shema, the great commandment of the Jewish law. There's something powerful and fundamental about it. There is an interesting thing, a surprising thing. Despite the unwavering biblical emphasis on the importance of the home... despite its centrality as the cradle of faith, good biblical examples of ideal family life are extraordinarily difficult to find.

Look at the first family in the garden. No work to do; no deadlines to meet. All their food was provided, gratis, they didn't need clothes, had eternal springtime, they were in paradise, a lifetime of pleasures.

Yet, look what they did with it; look what came out of it...
squabbling,
finger pointing,
mutual blaming,
dissolution and ultimate rejection, and the unspeakable
horror of losing one son at the hands of the other son.
Their story no more began than it fell apart.

Going a little farther down the line, we see Isaac and Rebekah played favorites between their twin boys—he spoiled one, she the other. Their actions drove a wedge between the sons, creating an enmity that lasted nearly a lifetime, and came within a whisker of derailing the plan of redemption.

King David's family life was almost a case study in how it *shouldn't* be done. If anybody ever tries to sell a book titled *Good Parenting and How I Achieved It*, written by King David, don't bother to buy it.

King David was great in many ways: a great warrior, a great motivator, and a great king. But his home was a mess. His own son started a revolution against him that almost toppled the kingdom. When he died, his body wasn't even cold before his heirs were infighting over the succession. I shudder to think what the *National Enquirer* would have done with it if it had been publishing in those days.

I know that sounds a little funny, but this old book is the most modern book ever written. Nothing really changes year after year, century after century, primarily because it's written about *people*. I think the Bible was written with ruthless honesty, not glossing over unpleasantness just because it *is* unpleasant, but rather laying it out openly so it can be dealt with...by us.

"These words, which I command thee this day, shall be in thine heart: and thou shalt teach them diligently unto thy children, and shalt talk of them when thy sittest in thy house" (Deut. 6:6–7). The sanity of the Bible is so clear and so compelling.

Dr. Elton Trueblood, the eminent Quaker theologian, once wrote, "No home is fully developed until the members of it recognize that the home, itself, is a religious institution."

I often wonder what a difference it would make if families who face serious strife and disagreements would address those situations with genuine prayer. I write this with almost a lump in my throat, not as one who can claim to have practiced it with my own family, but one who stands in awe before the seriousness of it. And it's never too late to start.

I love the early 1800s story about Brooke Adams. His father kept a daily diary. On one particular day, there was this brief notation, "Went fishing all day with my son...day wasted."

The son, young Brooke, also kept a diary. He also made an entry in his diary that particular day. When researchers checked the corresponding dates later, they found he had written, "My father took me fishing today. It was the most wonderful day of my life." You never know.

G. K. Chesterton used to say that nothing is more practical than a good theory. It's the admission of and a commitment to an acceptance of loyal discipline as the means of realizing the kind of fulfilling family God wants His children to experience. Everything worth doing, everything really significant, involves some hardship and usually involves self-denial...meaningful family life included. "I'd give *anything* for children like yours," an admiring woman said to a friend. To which the other woman replied, "I did."

I believe the writings of this austere book are put down to constantly remind us that there can be no true happiness, no family in any meaningful sense, without the loyal acceptance of discipline. I think the rules and regulations were put down as a map to guide us through the rough times.

"Hear, O Israel: The LORD our God is one LORD: And thou shalt love the LORD thy God with all thine heart, and with all thy soul, and with all thy might. And these words, which I command thee this day, shall be in thine heart: And thou shalt teach them diligently unto thy children, and shalt talk of them when thou sittest in thine house, and when thou walkest by the way, and when thou liest down, and when thou risest up. And thou shalt bind them for a sign upon thine hand, and they shall be as frontlets between thine eyes. And thou shalt write them upon the posts of thy house, and on thy gates" (Deut. 6:4–9).

chapter 13

FODDER WING

DEUTERONOMY 34:4, AMP

"And the Lord said to him, This is the land which I swore to Abraham,
Isaac, and Jacob, saying, I will give it to your descendants. I have
let you see it with your eyes, but you shall not go over there."

O N A VERY special Thanksgiving not long ago, my niece Trish and her
husband Ray traveled all the way to Florida from Alaska just to spend
one of their precious holidays with us away from their families they left behind
in Alaska. What a treat and gift for Sara and me that these two people would
think that much of us to do such an act of kindness.

As I marvel at the depth of this gesture, my mind drifts toward those small
things in our lives that oftentimes go unnoticed or are taken for granted. Moses
had such instances of God's love thrust into his path, and they, too, must have
gone unnoticed, or at least God may have seen it as such.

In some ways, it must have been a devastating disappointment...after all
that Moses had been through and now so close not to even be allowed to go
in. The Promised Land is what we're talking about here... Maybe he will get a
small glimpse at the promise through those one-hundred-twenty-year-old eyes.
It just didn't seem fair. We all like happy endings.

But Moses never got the satisfaction of setting one little toe on the
    ground that represented
      his goal,
        his dream,
          his obsession through all those long years of struggle,
            since God first called him in the burning bush, on the side
          of the mountain.

He had worked, sweat, argued, fought, and led his people out of slavery and performed almost an incomprehensible task of directing those thousands of complaining refugees in a journey across the desert. When they left Egypt, they were a motley aggregation of individuals, but by the time they reached Palestine, they had become a nation.

But here he is at the end of his journey. If he could just be allowed a little taste. Deuteronomy tells it best, I believe. In a matter-of-fact and straightforward way, the Lord simply took Moses up to the overlook there on the east side of the Jordan, Mt. Pisgah, turned him to the west, and gave him a look, nothing more. Then He took him home.

Somehow, though, in another sense, I don't really feel that sorry for Moses. Whoever in this life really gets more than a peek at the promise? And if the promise is big enough, isn't that enough? Isn't a peek enough to keep us going? I know raising four children—four peeks at a promise—is enough for me that my dreams will follow through. One's dreams ought to be more than what can be crammed into seventy or eighty or ninety years.

Peter Taylor Forsyth wrote in one of his books, "There are those who quietly say, as their faith follows their loved ones into the unknown, 'I know that land. I've never been there myself, but some of my people live there. They are gone abroad there on secret Foreign Service, which does not admit of communication. But I meet from time to time the commanding officer, and when I mention them to him, he assures me that all is well.'"

Having spent a full week in the hills of Tennessee with our grandchildren and watching them rollicking in all that that land affords a small child's imagination, my mind falls back to one of my favorite stories.

That story is by Marjorie Kinnan Rawlings, *The Yearling*. I'm sure most of you have read the book or at least seen the movie starring Gregory Peck. It's a novel about a primitive, backward people living in the late 1800s in Florida around the Ocala National Forest. In the movie, the one character who stands out and stays clean through all the hardships of the story is Penny, the father, played by Gregory Peck.

However, there is another character, a pitiful, crippled, half-wit boy by the name of Fodder Wing, whose very existence would seem to some a complaint against the goodness of God. But this child with a twisted body and a twisted mind had a way with animals, and all the little wild creatures became his friends.

Then comes the day when Fodder Wing dies. His body lies in the rough handmade casket, and his family and friends gather for the funeral. There is no preacher, but somehow people instinctively, at a time like that, turn toward the Creator. One of them said, "Penny, you've had some Christian raisin'. We'd be proud did you say something."

And Penny stands at the edge of the open grave and lifts up his face to the sunlight, and while the rough men around take off their hats and bow their heads, he offers up his prayer:

> O Lord, Almighty God. Hit ain't for us ignorant mortals to say what's right and what's wrong. Was ary one of us to be a-doin' it, we'd not a brung this pooo boy into the world a cripple, and his mind teched. We'd a brung him in straight and tall like his brothers... fittin' to live and work and do.
>
> But in a way of speakin', Lord, you done made it up to him. You give him a way with the wild critters. You give him a sort of wisdom, make him knowin' and gentle. The birds come to him, and the varmints moved free about him, and like as not he could have taken a wild she cat in them poor, twisted hands.
>
> Now you've done seen fit to take him where bein' crookedy in mind and limb don't matter. But, Lord, hit pleasures us to think now you've done straightened out them legs, and that poor bent back, and them hands. Hit pleasures us to think on him moving around as easy as anybody else.
>
> And Lord, give him a few red birds, and maybe a squirrel, and a coon, and a opossum to keep him company like he had down here. All of us is somehow lonesome, and we know he'll not be so lonesome do he have them little wild things around him, if it ain't askin' too much to put a few varmints in heaven. Amen.

Well, we all know there are a lot of disappointments and injustices in this life. However, much of God's mysterious ways we don't understand. I think something deep inside of us knows there is justice and basic goodness in the character of the Commanding Officer... and all is well.

As long as there are the Trish and Rays in the world, who *take the time*, there are children to carry on the dreams, there are the Moseses who stand on the slopes of Mt. Pisgah viewing Canaan. We know that we will always have a peek at the promise, and I think for now, it is enough.

chapter 14

SO WHAT IF WE AREN'T ALL ALIKE?

1 KINGS 19:9-12

"…and after the earthquake a fire…and after the fire a still small voice."

S TILL SMALL VOICE? What do you mean, still small voice? How could God be a still small voice? That's not where you find God. That's not how the Almighty reveals Himself.

It's in those other things—the earthquake, wind, and fire—where God is supposed to be. That's God's habitat; everybody knows that.

Still small voice, Elijah? Are you trying to pull something over on me? Who are you trying to kid? Hey, man, I've been around. I think I'd better tell you a thing or two, ol' boy. I have some doubts about your veracity, maybe even your sobriety. Still small voice.

Don't you see, Elijah? If you're telling the truth, you don't fit the pattern, that's conventional wisdom; that's established truth. Hey, if you don't believe me, ask your buddy Moses. What better authority can you have?

Isn't that where he found God that day on the side of the mountain? Same mountain, by the way. The bush was burning, but it didn't burn up. God was in that fire. And later, wasn't He in the wind that blew across the Red Sea and parted the waters to let the Hebrew children escape from Egypt? God was in that wind. Earthquake, wind, and fire, now abideth those three. In the Bible, they're practically synonymous with God.

And now here comes Elijah; Elijah the nonconformist,
    the misfit,
        the unconventional one,
            the oddball, saying,

"Hey, something different happened to me. I didn't experience God in the conventional way. I didn't find Him in earthquake, wind, or fire as those traditional forms of epiphany. To me God came as a still small voice, very quietly, very unobtrusively. I almost couldn't hear a thing. *But nothing could have been more real.*"

Now what do you think is the point here, lurking in the shadows? Could it be a biblical illustration of religious diversity, what the philosopher William James called "the variety of religious experience"? So what if we aren't all alike? Do we have to be? Does everybody have to fit the same mold? Do we all have to have the identical type of religious experience? Maybe there's room for a little more diversification than we think there is.

I'd like to call Elijah as a witness. He certainly didn't fit somebody else's mold. Let's face it, the boy was a strange duck, even by biblical standards.

The Bible, I think we would all agree, is full of eccentric people, different people, unusual people.

There are more rare individuals, more bizarre personalities, more colorful characters per square yard in the Bible than in any other collection of people I know anything about... except maybe the Congress of the United States.

But of all the colorful characters in this "book of colorful characters," I don't know of anybody more rare and bizarre than Elijah. Remember why he was in that cave on the side of the mountain? Remember how he got there? There had been a contest earlier on the top of Mt. Carmel, a battle of the gods, a duel of deities. You took your religion seriously in those days.

Yahweh, the Sovereign God of the Hebrews versus Baal, the Canaanite idol. Elijah, the lone representative of God, versus four hundred fifty of Queen Jezebel's finest, handpicked priests. It was a contest to see which god was stronger, which god could "cut it." Sort of an ancient world NBA playoff, an engagement to determine which god could first send fire raining down on the altar.

And what a show Elijah put on. I guess you could call him the P. T. Barnum of antiquity... He was Bill Cosby, Phil Donahue, and Moshe Dayan all rolled into one, with maybe a touch of Larry King thrown in for good measure. He was a showman, and he milked every ounce of drama he could from the situation.

The Baalites went first, working themselves into a frenzy, cutting themselves with knives, shouting, pleading, dancing around like dervishes, until they were totally exhausted, while Elijah sat on a rock nearby and snickered.

"What's the matter, boys? Having trouble? Where is your god? I don't believe I see him. Maybe he had to go to the bathroom." That's literally what the Hebrew text says, honest. And when they gave up in futility, and his turn came, Elijah really let 'em have it. "Pour water on the altar," he said. "Drench the wood, saturate it. My God will still send fire."

And He did! It was fantastic. Now I know the report is probably biased. We don't have a comparable account from the Baalite journalist who was covering the event for Jezebel. The report we do have was written for home consumption, but even taking that into account, it's impressive.

Why, the whole thing burned up. *Whoosh!* The flames even licked up the water they had poured into the trenches. The flames roared into the sky, proclaiming victory with every crackle. And when the humiliation was over, Elijah took the four hundred fifty priests of Baal down to the Brook of Kishon, and there he slew them. I don't know how or why they all waited around for this one man to kill the four hundred fifty, but that's what Scripture says.

In the meantime, Queen Jezebel heard about the incident. Four hundred fifty chaplains are one thing, but an irate woman is something else. And Jezebel was not your ordinary, run-of-the-mill, mousy little woman. Even her name was loathsome—*Jezebel*. You feel like you want to wash your mouth out after you pronounce it. That's the kind of woman she was.

When Jezebel found out what Elijah had done to her henchmen, she sat down at the mahogany desk over there at the palace and dashed off a note to him, saying, "Dear Elijah, greetings. How's the family? Wife and kids doing OK?" No, you're right. She didn't exactly write those words, but she did write these: "May the gods deal with me, be it ever so severely, if by this time tomorrow I do not make your life like that of one of them." (See 1 Kings 19:2.) Great! She's even precise about the exact hour, which heightened the terror.

So, here is Elijah, having fled the country, out in the wilderness, hiding in a cave, alone, frustrated, disappointed, frightened—on top one day and toppled the next. A commanding, undaunted champion one day, and a pitiful, dejected refugee the next. And that's when it happened.

In that setting of despondence and inadequacy, right then, when all the defenses were down and there was no place left to run, it was then that Elijah, the individual, had his special experience.

The truth is, I suppose, Elijah was in no condition for earthquake, wind, and fire. He was in no mental state for that. After all he'd been through, it would have blown his mind; it would have knocked him right off his pins.

But does it really matter? The point is not the method of His coming. The point has nothing to do with mechanics of His appearing. That's secondary. There's a deeper reality. So what if God didn't speak to Elijah the same way He did to Moses? Where does it say He has to?

What happened to the apostle Paul was different from what happened to Peter, and to John, and Pascal, and to Mother Teresa...but the Word was able to get through.

Martin Luther was literally thrown to the ground by a bolt of lightning during a thunderstorm.

Thomas Aquinas had his deepest revelation with God while sitting alone at his desk, writing a book.

What the passage is trying to say is, don't be too quick to judge somebody else's religious experience, or your own, for that matter. Leave room in your expectations for God to work the way He wants to work.

What a liberating thought. You don't have to be what you're *not* to be a Christian.

chapter 15

WHERE WERE YOU...? WHERE *ARE* YOU?

JOB 38:4, AMP

"Where were you when I laid the foundation of the earth?"

WHAT A WONDERFUL, thought-inspiring book the Book of Job is, then and now. It contains so many insightful messages. It would take more than a year, or a lifetime, to uncover all that it contains for our present-day lives.

As I read it again, I am reminded of one of Thornton Wilder's brilliant little miniplays titled *An Angel That Troubled the Waters*. It's fewer than three pages long, and the setting is the Pool of Siloam in Jerusalem, where a host of wounded, crippled, and sick persons are waiting for the waters to stir so they can throw themselves in and be cured.

A newcomer arrives to stand among the waiting. His hurt is not external, of the flesh, but is inward, piercing his soul. He prays, "O God, how heavy my heart is. I am weighted down by the burden and hurts I've experienced. If only I could be cured of this inner pain. Then I would be free to be of more service to You."

Just then the angel appears, the waters stir, and the physically sick leap into the pool, each trying to be first. But the Angel restrains the newcomer, holding him back, saying, "Friend, healing is not for you." "What do you mean, not for me? Think what I might do in love's service were I but freed of this bondage."

The angel stands a moment in silence, then answers, "Without your wound, where would your power be? The very angels of heaven cannot persuade the wretched and blundering children of earth as can one human being broken on the wheels of living. In love's service, only the wounded soldier can serve."

There is a story about Carlisle Anderson, missionary to China, who was imprisoned by the Red Army when they took over that country. They didn't abuse him physically, but they just stuck him away in solitary confinement for two years. At first, Anderson said, he felt desperately sorry for himself; after all, he was just thirty-five years old. He had a wife and two children back home. He'd been a good Christian. He'd taken a salary most of us would have thought indecent. Then, after all that sacrifice, all that he had given up to try and help them, the Chinese themselves didn't appreciate him. They just locked him up without a trial, and without even telling him the charges against him. For a long time, Anderson spun a cocoon of self-pity around himself, and he became lonelier and lonelier.

One day, Carlisle Anderson had the grace to look at his situation from a different perspective.

Almost out of the blue, he said, it came to him with force of revelation. Instead of asking, "Why did this happen to me?" He began to ask, "Well, why shouldn't this happen to me? Why should I be exempt? After all, I'm a Christian; the Reds aren't. I'm supposed to be a believer; the Reds make no pretense of it. It's really a compliment to the work I was doing that they wanted to get rid of me. If Christianity is what I believe it is and Communism is what I believe it to be, then why shouldn't I be in jail?"

The cocoon broke, he said, when he realized that. He had a whole new outlook, a whole new frame of reference. He'd turned his loneliness into an asset because he had found that even under those circumstances, his witness could still have an impact.

Up to this point in the Old Testament writings, we have seen time and time again when we mess up, God is right there to deal with the situation, oftentimes with an iron fist. Even in the Book of Job, Job's buddies were anxious to point out to him that, due to the plight that he was in, he must have really done something wrong to upset God. "So, Job, what did you do?" his friends asked. "Come on now, ol' boy, fess up."

I think if we learn anything at all from the Bible, it makes abundantly clear that God is the same then and now and for all time to come. God does not change. He only changes the way in which He deals with His people.

In Proverbs 3:11–12, we read, "My son, do not despise or shrink from the chastening of the Lord...neither be weary of...His reproof, for whom the Lord loves He corrects, even as a father corrects the son in whom He delights" (AMP).

When I was just a little boy, my father and I would sometimes tussle on the floor, as fathers and sons often do. I did the same thing with my children a generation later. Because my father was obviously bigger and stronger than I was then, every once in a while in the process of playing around together, there were times when he inadvertently inflicted pain on me.

Sometimes, of course, there were other occasions where he inflicted pain on purpose. Like most of you, I'm sure, I had my share of the willow branch treatment. Actually for me, it was an oak tree in our backyard. I swear that Dad planted that tree there for the sole purpose of having his own personal stash of switches. "Dale, take my pocket knife and go cut me a switch. And don't bring back one that will break easily, or when I finish breaking that one on you, I'll go cut my own." Ironically, when my last sibling passed away last January, that knife was the only thing that I received from either of my parents. To this very day, when I get near an oak tree, my legs break out in whelps.

Those are two contrasting kinds of experiences. Sometimes I received pain administered deliberately, while on other occasions pain was delivered accidently. There was pain and suffering under both circumstances, maybe as much when it was caused by accident as when it was inflicted by mere circumstance.

There was a major difference, and I can remember that difference. The pain didn't feel the same when I looked up into my father's eyes, saw the dark cloud of parental disapproval, and knew he meant business. The pain was much worse, and tears would correspondingly flow unabated.

When I looked up at my father and knew that he was just playing, that he didn't mean to hurt me, and that he, too, was bothered by my pain, somehow it didn't hurt as much.

Isn't the same thing true on a larger scale as well? How in the world did ol' Job keep his wits about him out there on the dung heap?

After he had lost everything?
After he was left with just his racked body, covered with boils?

It took him a while, but in the end Job consulted the eyes of his heavenly Father and realized that in spite of the bitterness of it, his suffering was not really God's intention. It was there, but God was with him in it.

We may not always be able to understand the "why" of certain things that happen to us. We can't always tell why this thing or that thing occurred, but we see through the message of this ancient book and can be comforted by knowing that God does not intend our suffering. When we look up into His face and see that His sympathy and concern are not against us but with us and for us, it somehow makes what we have to bear not quite so harsh.

No one would ever be so crass to imply that suffering is good, but sometimes good can come out of it. The Arabs have a saying: "All sunshine makes a desert." I suppose the point of this saying is that into each life a little rain had better fall or that life is likely to end up, metaphorically, like the Dead Sea, which is capable of receiving only unto itself and not producing anything living.

Helen Keller was asked about all the roadblocks that had been thrown in her path, and why they hadn't made her bitter. Her response was, "The truth is I believe that what happens to you in life is probably not nearly as important as how you react to what happens to you."

Certainly the sufferings and tragedy of life are hard to bear. We can't always explain them, and we often can't understand them. When we try to run away from them and blame God in the process, we only add insult to injury.

I think it all comes down to the very core of our faith. I can almost see Paul, pausing with quill in hand, making sure he hadn't left anything out when he was writing to the Romans. "What shall separate us from the love of God? Shall tribulation, distress, persecution, famine, nakedness or sword? Neither death or life nor angels nor principalities nor powers nor things present nor things to come."

Nowhere in the Bible does it tell us that we are going to be excluded from the pain that comes with this journey called life. All we can do is to be like Paul when he wrote, "In all situations I find myself, I will give praise to God."

chapter 16

THE PREACHER WHO SUCCEEDED...AND FAILED

JONAH 3:1–5; 4:1—11, AMP
"Arise, go to Nineveh, that great city, and preach and
cry out to it the preaching that I tell you."

THE STORY BEGINS by God calling Jonah: "Arise, go to Nineveh, that great city, and cry against it, for their wickedness has come up before me." Now Nineveh was the capital city of Assyria, just north of present-day Iraq. Ninevites were the archenemies, the implacable foes of all that Judaism stands for. And God wanted Jonah to go and preach a little to them, tell them where they had gone wrong.

And what did Jonah do when he got the call? What does any red-blooded patriotic prophet do when God lays a burden like that on his heart? *He runs!* He runs away as fast as his little legs can churn.

You really need a map to appreciate where that boy went. Jonah was in Judah, eastern end of the Mediterranean. Nineveh, where God wanted him to go, was way farther east. So, direction-challenged Jonah headed west in the exact opposite direction. He went to Joppa, on the coast, hopped a freighter, and sailed to Tarshish on the other end of the Mediterranean. Tarshish was in Spain, for heaven's sake.

Jonah didn't trust God to do with the Ninevites what Jonah thought God should do. If he could really be sure that God would hold the line, be severe and judgmental with His punishment, well, maybe he would have gone. "Now God, You know I don't like those people, and I could go preach them a little sermon like You want me to, but what if they actually repent? Would You let them off the hook? If that's Your intention, then count me out."

So Jonah ran. I think it was Charlie Brown, the sage and wise seer of all things, who once said, "No problem is so big that you can't run away from it." But what do you do, if *you* are the problem? How and where and from whom do you run?

Now, here comes the greatness of God: He didn't let him get away. Jonah ran, but God brought him back kicking and screaming. Jonah may have given up on the Ninevites, but God hadn't given up on him. Theologian and author Francis Thompson calls it "the relentless hound of heaven those strong feet, following, following after." God let Jonah run, but He stayed right with him.

I believe the storm at sea that followed, the storm that nearly ripped the ship apart, is the story of God's pursuit of a fugitive. Like most characters depicted in the Bible, there was as much a storm inside of Jonah as there was on the outside. Then Jonah did the most noble, the most grand the most hypocritical thing: "Throw me into the sea, and the sea will quiet down for you. For I know it is because of me that this has come to you."

He would have rather died than admit what he was running from, that he may just be on the same level as the ones he was to minister to. Nothing ministers to one's pride quite like being a martyr. "I'll take the blame. You guys go ahead without me." So they tossed him into the drink.

Now, I have researched all the different versions of the Bible that I have in my possession, and it doesn't refer to it as a whale. It's a *big fish*. And if you are a fisherman (or a fisherwoman), you know how those fish stories can be. In fact, the Fisherman's Information Bureau in Chicago registers the catches of large and record-sized fish with the initials FIB.

At any rate, Jonah knew at last that he couldn't escape. His heart wasn't in his mission, but he arrived in Ninevah and hoped they wouldn't listen. Can't you just imagine what was going on in his mind, especially after riding around the ocean inside a fish for three days?

> He walked through the city for three days...
> from one end to the other just glaring at people,
> operating out of duty but not out of compassion,
> doing a job, but grinding his teeth,
> preaching to their faces but despising their hearts.

His sermon was just eight words long. *Eight words!* "Yet forty days, and Nineveh shall be overthrown" (Jon. 3:4).

Jonah's deepest fears, his darkest suspicions, materialized from those eight words. A revival swept the city, from person to person, block to block. Jonah had to step back out of the way to keep from being trampled. Everybody in town put on sackcloth and ashes, turned the direction of their lives around, and fell on their knees. The people had heard the voice of God even through the despicable attitude of a preacher.

And for the second time in the story, Jonah assumed the role of the wounded martyr. "If You're not going to let me watch You wreak vengeance on my enemies, I'd rather die than live."

We are told that Jonah is sitting on the side of a hill, overlooking the city. We're even told more; it's on the *east* side of the hill, the far side, where he can look down and across, over the town and beyond the town, in the direction of Judah toward *home.* He's eating his heart out, frustrated, remorseful, hurt, and angry. He won...but he lost. He was successful, in a sense, but a failure.

But, one more chance for the old boy. Here is the climax of the story. God, in His ever-reaching patience, sent a plant, a fast-growing plant, to grow over Jonah's head to provide shade for him from the broiling sun. The Hebrew Bible identifies the plant as the castor plant; yes, that's where we get castor oil. What a perfect remedy for such a poop-head. If only he had eaten the plant instead of getting shade from it. He was that close.

Now, if you think about it, everybody else in the story—the sailors, the citizens of Nineveh, even the fish all of them—came off smelling better than Jonah did. Even the castor tree God sent is attacked by a worm and withers and dies. And the morose old moralist resumes his previous coloration; he goes back to pouting, saying once more, "It is better for me to die, rather than to live."

The story draws to a close with just one more stab from God: "Jonah, Jonah, you pity the plant for which you did not labor, nor did you make it grow, which came into being in a night, and perished in a night. Should not I pity Nineveh, that great city, where there are more than a hundred twenty thousand persons who do not know their right hand from their left?" (See Jonah 4:10.) The curtain drops, and the point is made.

The world appears always to be in chaos regardless of the age, so we need to revisit this old book to remind us of the *point* again. The love of God, undiluted and unending, is for all, the deserving, the undeserving, the just and the unjust...

the Jews,
   the Ninevites,
      the Christians,
        the Muslims,
          us,
            and them.

chapter 17

IT WAS (YOU MIGHT SAY) SATISFACTORY

MATTHEW 2:9

"And, lo, the star, which they saw in the east, went before them."
Lines found in T. S. Elliot's poem, "Journey of the Magi," describe the
rigors of the trip across the continent—the freezing temperatures, the
inconvenience, the duplicity of the camel drivers: "A cold time we had
of it." The climax is told so simply, so matter-of-factly, it's almost anti-
climactic: "And so we continued, and arrived at evening, not a moment
too soon, finding the place; it was (you might say) satisfactory."

SATISFACTORY! CAN YOU believe that? Talk about understatement. Why
didn't he say overwhelming or fulfilling or stupendous? "It was (you might
say) satisfactory." Well, I guess it was.

"And lo, the star, which they saw in the east, went before them, until it came
to rest over the place where the child was." So Matthew reported. They had
arrived, and it was "satisfactory."

The timing and location of the event is even more of a mystery. Why there?
Why then? The location of it seems strange, don't you think? Born in Bethlehem of Judea, of all places. And of course the *how* of it sends your mind
absolutely reeling: "Born of a virgin by the Holy Spirit." I guess the details, the
particulars, the specifics of the event seem somehow more manageable, even
more fitting, when you are grasped by the size and scope of the heart behind
it all. If you can accept that there is a *why* to the story, you can accept the rest
with relative ease.

Actions, both good and evil, largely are the fruit of intent. Jesus obviously
knew that. "Out of the heart are the issues of life," He said. "As he thinks in
his heart, so is he" (Prov. 23:7, AMP). He knew that if people wanted the right
things, they'd allow those wants to lead them to the right choices.

All of Scripture is a mystery at first in our journey, and no matter how hard we try, we can't explain a mystery. A preacher may be fully prepared to deliver his or her message, but we, the hearer, will receive it the way God wants us to hear it...when we are ready.

At the very heart of our belief is the conviction that God beckons, takes the initiative, invites, and calls us to respond, and the restlessness of the heart bears witness to it. I think Matthew tells it best: "And lo, the *star*, which they saw in the east, went before them" (Matt. 2:9). Who knows what it really was, that famous *star* of Bethlehem?

Matthew reports it.
   Christmas art depicts it.
      Tradition cherishes it.

Does it even matter all that much what it really was? There's something a lot bigger here than mere fact; isn't it often so? When you've explained the biology of human birth, have you explained birth? I feel we're talking more than astronomy. Even Bethlehem itself is more than geography, and the manger more than wood.

The star was not only there at the start; it was there along the way. Matthew says it went before them, guiding them, accompanying them from start to finish. There is purpose in the journey itself, it says to us. In the very act of faithful following, even if it means taking only tiny steps at first, comes growth and maturity.

It is probably not without significance in the story that the wise men were not natives of Bethlehem. The Savior wasn't born in the town where they lived. There was something they had to *do* to get to Him. The journey of spiritual maturity is not a matter of finding the nearest shortcut; neither is it a matter of opting for easy designations. God doesn't trample on our freedoms. He never makes us go, but we must decide whether to stay where we are...or journey.

Somewhere in one of his many books, author Clovis Chappell tells the story of a fourth wise man at Christmas who saw, but did not follow, the star.

He wanted to go, all right. He rejoiced in the news of the announcement, talked with the others, made plans, and wrestled with the options.

But when it came down to it, he stayed behind and didn't make the journey.

Years later, as an old man, he held his little grandchild on his knee and told him the stirring story of that night, when the others had set out on their quest.

When he finished, the little boy's eyes widened, and he said, "Well, is that all, Grandpa? Is that all there is? Was the Christ child really born?" The old man shook his head sadly and said, "I never knew. Some say it was true. Some say it was only a dream. I didn't take the trouble to go see."

Part of the wonder and mystery of the star is its accompanying *grace*. When we follow it, we get more light. Each time we take a step, even a small one, each time we step out in faith, new light comes from the taking of the next.

The star is there to get us started, it's there to guide us as we go, and it's there waiting for us when we arrive at journey's end.

George Buttrick in the *Interpreter's Bible* reports an old legend that traditionally has been attributed to Marco Polo. In the legend, all the wise men came from the same town, a small village in Persia. There were three of them—a young man, a middle-aged man, and an older man. The young man found, so the legend says, a young Christ, the man of middle years found a Christ his own age, and the older man found Christ *an old companion*.

Sometimes legends contain truth then goes beyond truth. Each person finds his true life in Christ. The *star of Bethlehem* represents the goal of all our searching, the balm of all our aching, the clue to the solution of all our wondering, and the rest at last we seek for all our *wandering*.

It is said that at the end of the First World War, a French soldier was found suffering from amnesia. When he was picked up at a railroad station, he looked at his questioners blankly and all he could say was, "I don't know who I am. I don't know who I am." Because he had been disfigured by facial wounds, there were three different families who claimed him as belonging to them. He was taken from village to village where the families lived and allowed to walk around by himself. When he entered the third village, a sudden light of recognition came to his eyes. He walked down a side street, in through a tiny gate, and up the steps of his father's house. Like the Prodigal Son, he had come to his senses. The old familiar surroundings had restored his mind once again, he knew who he was, and to whom he belonged.

But isn't this just like *Christmas*? Many of us are like amnesia victims. We have forgotten who we really are and to whom we really belong. When we hear once again the old, yet ever so new, story of Bethlehem, when we follow the star God put in the sky and let it lead us through the streets of life, we know somehow that we have found our way *home*.

chapter 18

REROUTED FISHERMEN

MATTHEW 4:19

"Follow me, and I will make you fishers of men."

So MANY QUESTIONS inevitably jump out at us when we think of Jesus choosing His disciples. Had He known them before this encounter? What do you suppose Zebedee must have thought? And Mrs. Zebedee, for crying out loud, when he got home and tried to explain it? We don't know the answers to those questions. The first chosen were perfectly average, normal people.

Somebody, with tongue in cheek, constructed a memo made up to look as if it had come from a First Century Management Consulting Firm evaluation of the twelve disciples. It's addressed to Jesus, Son of Joseph and Woodcrafters Carpenter Shop of Nazareth.

"Dear Sir, Thank you for submitting the resumes of the twelve men you have picked for managerial positions in your organization. All of them have now taken our battery of tests, and we have not only run the results through our computer, but also arranged personal interviews for each of them with our psychologists and our vocational aptitude people.

"It is the staff's opinion that most of your nominees are lacking in background, education, and vocational aptitude for the type of enterprise you are undertaking. They do not have the team concept. We would recommend that you continue your search for persons of experience in managerial ability and proven capacity.

"Simon Peter is exceptionally unstable and given to fits of temper. Andrew has absolutely no qualities of leadership. The two brothers, James and John, the sons of Zebedee, place personal interests above company loyalty. Thomas demonstrates a questionable attitude that would tend to undermine morale. We feel it is our duty to tell you that Matthew has been blacklisted by the Greater Jerusalem Better Business Bureau. James, the son of Alphaeus, and

Thaddeus definitely have radical leanings, and they both register high scores on the manic-depressive scale.

"One of the candidates, however, shows great potential. He is a man of ability and resourcefulness, meets people well, has a keen business mind, and has contacts in high places. He is highly motivated, ambitious, and responsible. We recommend Judas Iscariot as your comptroller and right-hand man. All the other profiles are self-explanatory.

"We wish you every success in your new venture.

Sincerely yours."

Notice what the disciples were doing when Jesus encountered them. They were engaged in their daily work. In this case, they were mending their nets. That's when the Lord fingered them.

As far as we know they weren't thinking about spiritual matters when it happened. They were engrossed in thinking about holes and needles and thread and getting the job done so they could get back to business. It was when they least expected it that He collared them.

The good news is that God doesn't have to work through some preplanned, predescribed scheme or revelation. He has a huge box of innovative initiatives, and your experience doesn't have to be the same as somebody else's. Here He calls these first disciples while they are busy in a secular job.

How did Browning put it?

Just when we are safest, there's a sunset-touch,
  A fancy from a flower-bell, some one's death,
    A chorus-ending from Euripides—
      And that's enough for fifty hopes and fears
        As old and new at once as nature's self,
          To rap and knock and enter in our soul.[1]
            That's it. You never know.

Before He asked anything else of them, He asked them simply to follow. That's it. "Follow Me," He said, and immediately they left their nets and followed Him.

That's how it started. Instruction, training, deepening theological understanding—all that would come in time, but He didn't make it a prerequisite for initiating the pilgrimage.

For Jesus, discipleship was a way of life before it was anything else. It's how you begin, not how you end up. You must first make the decision to follow.

Notice who they were, notice what they were doing, and notice what He asked them to do. But most importantly notice what He offered them when He called them to begin. He offered them *Himself.* "Follow Me."

What makes it so meaningful, so rewarding, and so impossible to abandon for those who have started the journey is the privilege of simply being in His presence.

He never offered us exemption or immunity from hardship, suffering, or pain, just as He never offered it to those first disciples. But if we truly want to be His disciple, if we want to live, really live, we need to hear His invitation clearly: "Follow Me, and I will make you."

chapter 19

WHEN MOURNING COMES

MATTHEW 5:4

"Blessed are they that mourn: for they shall be comforted."
Every time the anniversary of our nation's tragedy of September 11
rolls around, we all listen and watch as we individually deal with
this dark and tragic day. How our hearts still go out to those families and heroes during the anniversary of their loss.

IN THE FIFTH chapter of the Book of Matthew, Jesus delivers the Beatitudes to the multitude. Here lie the startling words of Jesus Himself as He addresses mourning: *"Blessed are those who mourn, for they shall be comforted."*

If these words had not come from Jesus, it might almost be suspect. It's contrary to common sense, so opposite to what you would expect.

Blessed means "to be given to" and *beatus*, according to my limited knowledge of Latin, literally means "happy." If He wanted to be realistic, why didn't Jesus say, "Blessed are those who don't have to mourn"? That would make more sense, I think.

Why didn't He say, "Blessed are those who go through life entirely in the sunshine"?

Why didn't He say, "Blessed are those whose eyes are never filled with tears"? Wouldn't that have been better?

It's what we work for, sacrifice for, what we want for ourselves and for our children and grandchildren. Why didn't He say, "Blessed are those who are fortunate enough to avoid completely the dark, forbidding shadows, who are immune from having to choke on their own tears, who can live all the way through this thing called life without ever having to experience hurt, the wrenching numbness that comes with the loss of a loved one"? *Why didn't He say something like that?*

But He didn't. He didn't say what *we* might expect, what seems natural to *us* and obvious and right. We all come to this life-wrenching **truth** about pain and suffering that, if we live long enough, we will have to endure.

He just doesn't seem to see the hurt that is caused by all this. When He comes up with strange paradoxical, unsettling things, that cut like a sword across our accepted values, it totally goes against our human understanding of the word *blessings*. Blessed, happy, fortunate. *What in the world was He thinking about when He said this?*

But I don't think Jesus ever meant to imply that mourning, in its many forms, is a blessing. I don't think that's good New Testament interpretation. Jesus never accepted a bad thing as a good thing. He never prescribed grief for its educational value. I think that would really be barbaric. He spent His life opposing human misery, human sadness.

He himself, as you recall, mourned with a deep-seated emotion at the loss of a friend. Jesus is reported as crying twice in the Gospels. Over the beloved city of Jerusalem He cried, "O Jerusalem, Jerusalem...How often would I have gathered your children together as a mother fowl gathers her brood under her wings, and you refused!" (Matthew 23:37 AMP). The other time was over the death of his friend Lazarus. John recounts it so well: "Jesus wept" (John 11:35). He cried real, physical, painful tears. Certainly that was not a blessing, not a "good" thing.

The loss of a loved one is, without debate or question, the most mind- and body-numbing emotion that mankind will ever have to deal with. And regardless of who it is that attempts to console you, there is no physical, emotional, or spiritual help that can allow you to see the significance of this waste of the most precious possession you have.

But after a while, after the blame subsides, after all the questions as to the *why*, we ask ourselves this question: where were we, within the Scriptures, promised escape from the pain or trouble or total confusion that all humans endure? We were never promised immunity from this pain and sorrow. Nobody can expect that. We will all mourn; we will all feel the pain eventually. It hurts, all right. Anybody who has ever been there knows it. It hurts like HELL!

But, I've learned of a medicine—an antidote, a resource—and it's tied up with that magnificent word *comfort*. It's laced all through the Book of Acts— through the rest of the Bible, for that matter: "Comfort ye, comfort ye my people" (Isa. 40:1); "Thy rod and thy staff they comfort me" (Ps. 23:4); and here's the kicker, "I will not leave you comfortless" (John 14:18).

I think what we do with the Bible, especially the Beatitudes, is we stop short. We don't read all the way through. "Blessed are those who mourn for they shall be comforted." That's the part we need to remember. We could actually call the Bible the Book of Comfort. One of its major themes is the loving support God wants to bestow on those who must pick up the pieces ripped apart by the experience of grief.

Although, I think there's more to this, I think we need also to focus on one important aspect: "Blessed are those who mourn, for they shall be comforted" *with a presence*. Remember in the Book of Daniel? Those three Hebrew boys found themselves thrown into the fiery furnace by the Babylonian king.

They were sheltered somehow, protected in their ordeal by the presence of Someone else. Someone else was right there with them. The prologue is almost like something out of Auschwitz...thrown into the furnace and abandoned. Yet they weren't abandoned. In the end the king says, "Did we not throw three men into the fire? I see four men loose, and they have no hurt, and the form of the fourth is like unto the Son of God." (See Daniel 3:24–25.)

Is this meant to be literal language or picture language? Well, I don't know that it matters. The *truth* is real. Someone else was in there with them. That's the point of it. In that desperate moment, that crisis moment, when it seemed there was no future, the presence of another broke through to uphold them.

I remember the *presence* quite clearly, quite distinctly, standing alongside the coffin of my son Ryan. I don't talk about it much because it's a very personal thing, but I remember it clearly. At the grave, Dr. Price read the familiar words from John, "I am the resurrection and the life....because I live, ye shall live also." When he said those words, it was as if Jesus Himself were saying them. *He was there!*

The reality of it didn't assuage the pain entirely; it certainly didn't remove it. It hurt just as much. But someone else was there too, and with that presence came the assurance that I could make it.

If you want an explanation, I can't give it. If you want to call it an illusion or self-hypnotic suggestion, I'm not in a mood to argue. I only know I was comforted. I was aware of a presence beyond me that came and strengthened and blessed.

St. Francis wrote in the hymn attributed to him, "And thou, most kind and gentle Death, waiting to hush our latest breath...Thou leadest home the child of God, and Christ our Lord the way hath trod."[1]

Someone else, who has been there before us, is there with us. That presence, in the midst of our mourning, won't remove the hurt, but it can lift us beyond it.

Out of mourning can come blessing, provided we allow it to help us catch a vision of what is really important, what is really worth our time and effort. Mourning is not good in itself. But out of it comes an appreciation for the real meaning of life:

> What is trivial subsides, and what is valuable…emerges.
> What is little fades, and what is big….blossoms.

It's almost as if Jesus is saying, "Out of your personal grief, your mourning, your sense of rejection, if you'll let it, there can come a new strength that can make you more of a complete person for *Me*."

It's not to say that brokenness and mourning are good in themselves. It's to say that *out* of them can come a heightened sensitivity that God can use in the service of others. You can use your hurt to make you a better healer, and you'll be empowered in the process.

When we finally make it to the bottom of our life, we think, "What else is there?" But there is still a promise, a promise from God. It comes from the One whose promises never fail. It comes as radiant assurance that our loved ones, who are separated from us now, will not be separated from us forever. A promise that, regardless of what gloom we perceive ourselves in, what obstacles seem to be constantly hurled in our path, there is still the promise!

Jesus said, "In my Father's house are many mansions: if it were not so I would have told you. I go to prepare a place for you" (John 14:2). Does it matter, really, whether we have a lot of details? Is that so important of how He's going to do it? I just can't get all that excited, frankly, about those physical descriptions of heaven that focus on golden streets and pearly gates and all that kind of splendor.

I don't believe, to be totally honest, that John, Milton, and Dante or anyone else knows enough to be that specific. I rather suspect we'll all be in for some surprises…but I think I know *why* they wrote.

They were trying to express the inexpressible. They were trying to convey what can't be adequately conveyed. They were trying somehow to put into finite words something mere words can't wrap around. What they were trying their level best to say is, "It's going to be wonderful."

It's a promise from the One who knew God better than anybody. So our mourning now, though painful, though real, though excruciatingly wrenching, is not a permanent thing.

God is with us now and has always been, and the good news is, He'll be with us at homecoming time. Like the father of the Prodigal Son, He'll be out there on the road as we arrive, to throw His arms around us and dress us up, to bring us to the feast and the glorious reunion.

"Let not your hearts be troubled." As historian and adventurer David Livingstone said with all the elegance of nineteenth-century British civility, "That's the promise of a gentleman." A gentleman who can honestly say, "I truly know exactly how you feel, and I'm right here when you need Me."

chapter 20

THE LITTLE SEED THAT COULD

MATTHEW 13:31–32, 44—52, AMP

"The kingdom of heaven is like a grain of mustard seed...it is the smallest, but
when it has grown it is the largest of the garden herbs and becomes a tree."

Do you know what I almost wish? Well, not quite, maybe, but *almost*.
I almost wish people didn't know the Bible so well. That may sound
strange, I mean, to wish for such a thing, but I do. I really do wish that people
didn't know the Bible so well.

Most of us have just enough familiarity with it to keep us from hearing what
it really says. It's as if we've been inoculated against catching an unadulterated
dose. I teach a thirty-two-week Bible class called Disciple. It goes from Disciple
I to Disciple IV. It covers 85 percent of the Bible, both New and Old Testaments. At the beginning of each fall session, potential inductees will come up
to me and tell me that they don't need to take the class again. They have already
taken it. When I hear those words, I wonder, "Do you read the Bible once like
a good mystery novel and put it up on the shelf never to open it again? Let it lie
there and collect dust?"

How so very different it must have been in the beginning. When Jesus spoke,
people listened. He spoke with freshness and intensity...and with sharpness
that caught people off guard by stabbing them with such honesty that they
could do nothing but listen.

Jesus spoke about things that were interesting because *He* was interesting.
He spoke about things that were familiar and commonplace, yet He gave them
a twist so that people saw them with new eyes. He opened windows for people
so that new light could shine in on their perspective and a fresh air could blow
through their experience.

Matthew captures many of these stories Jesus told. We call them parables,
though they are not all true parables in the technical sense. I'm sure if you

checked with your local resident English teacher, she may call them similes. They're not all complete stories as such; a parable usually is a story with a point.

Many of these stories are too brief, too compact for that…just flashes of insight. But through a sudden comparison, a quickly painted verbal picture, a telling phrase, Jesus lights up some aspect of truth.

> His illustrations don't explain so much as they stimulate or kindle.
> They don't analyze so much as they illuminate.
> They don't make us know more so much as they make us see more.
> They don't offer depth of information so much as they offer a burst of perception.
> You read them or hear them and say, "Of course. That's the way it is."

In the thirteenth chapter of Matthew, Jesus talks about the kingdom of God, or heaven, as Matthew preferred to call it. Not a place, but a relationship. It speaks to the rule of God, the reign of God, the sovereignty of God, over a life or over a situation.

What is that rule like when it comes to you, when you allow it to happen? It's like a treasure of enormous value, something worth giving up everything else; you have to possess it. Like a *pearl* of incomparable worth…*that* valuable!

Now we know none of the parables we read in the Gospels represent a complete picture of kingdom life. They don't embrace all of Christianity. You can't build a whole theology out of any one picture. Each suggests and contributes many different aspects to give us a clearer picture of God's truth.

I suppose no figure of speech Jesus ever used is more familiar to His people than the figure of the mustard seed. We all know the story, even if you don't know the plant. Most Christians were raised on this story.

In Luke 17:6 we read, "If ye had faith as a grain of mustard seed, ye might say unto this sycamine tree, Be thou plucked up by the root, and be thou planted in the sea; and it should obey you." That kind of story could really impress a little boy or girl when they read it.

Matthew's version of that passage turns the mulberry tree into a mountain. Not a bad piece of work for a mustard seed–sized faith. Do you know how big a mustard seed is? Well, if you were to hold a mustard seed between your thumb and index finger and walk to one side of the room and hold it up where someone on the other side could see it, they would probably doubt that you had anything between your fingers at all.

"What do mean you can't see it? Clean your glasses." *And, that's exactly the point!*

The author Fred Craddock reminds us that in the Gospels the placement of a story in the sequence of the material is often important...what comes before it and what follows it.

I think Jesus is trying to tell us that in our Christian walk, there are going to be times when you are not going to triumph. You're just not going to win them all. Not all the seeds you sow will fall on fertile ground; you might as well accept it. By the way, there are weeds out there. They're plentiful, and they're poisonous. You might as well accept that, too.

I think this story of the mustard seed is a realistic message that is hard-nosed and just plain spoken. This is how it is in life. Being in the kingdom doesn't make us exempt from hardship, it doesn't protect us from disaster or mourning, it doesn't guarantee us preferential treatment. To be honest, it may not make life any easier for you at all.

We do have one thing that is for certain. We have a *promise*—a cross-your-heart-and-hope-to-die pledge—to step over the line and into the kingdom. When you allow God to come first in your life, powerful, dynamic, transforming things will begin to happen. I think that's just about how the kingdom works. "The kingdom of heaven is like a mustard seed..."

You don't have to do something big and momentous to make a difference. What a relief to ordinary people like me. It doesn't take vast sums of money or time or ability or training to bring about positive change. All it takes is giving God a toehold in your life...providing Him with an opening through which to squeeze and offering Him even a minuscule-sized seed to take and run with. Invest a penny with God, and He'll break the bank.

In one of his famous writings, John Claypool uses an illustration taken from an old forties movie, *Stars in My Crown*. Dr. Claypool writes about an old Black man who lived all his life in a little town somewhere in the rural South and had been sort of an Uncle Remus to several generations of children in that area.

This man told the children stories, taught them to hunt, fish, and in general was greatly beloved. He owned a little cabin and some land, and after his wife died, he continued to live there alone. One year, a very valuable deposit of copper was discovered that ran through his property. Some business leaders of the town came to him and offered to buy his land. The old man wasn't from a money culture. He simply wanted to live out his days in the only house he had ever known, so he refused to sell.

A lot of money was at stake for the entire town, and the atmosphere turned ugly. When the businessmen could not buy him out, they resorted to nasty threats. Many of the very people he had befriended all his life became his foes. They sent him notes saying, "If you are not off the property by sundown tomorrow night, we are going to get you and hang you."

But one man in town, a lawyer, got wind of what was going on and went out to the old man's house. At the appointed hour, the would-be executioners rode up, hiding behind their white hoods and masks.

The lawyer stepped out onto the porch of the Black man and said, "John is aware of your intentions to hang him so he asked me to help him make out his will. He wants me to read it to you. First of all, he gives his fishing rod to Pete, because he remembers the first bass Pete caught with it. Next, he wants to give his rifle to James, because he remembers using it to teach him to shoot."

Item by item the old gentleman proceeded to give, in love, to the very people who had come to take his life. The impact of that was more than even their hardened spirits could handle. One by one, the would-be executioners turned away in silence until no one was left.

The old man's little grandson who had been watching the drama unfold from a distance came running into his grandfather's arms and asked, "What kind of will was that?" The old grandfather answered gently, "It was the will of God, son. The will of God."

It doesn't always end that happily and that smoothly, of course. In the movies, you can compress time, you have control over the plot, and you can even trim away all the loose edges. In the kingdom of God, however, even greater things are possible.

In a deeper sense, I guess, that's the story of the mustard seed, the power of God to do the impossible, the unlikely...the unbelievable through the tiny opportunities of faith that we show.

The binding pledge is that our mustard seed–sized faith, even that, can contribute to God's ultimate victory.

chapter 21

THE POWER OF A CRY

MATTHEW 15:21—38

"But she came and, kneeling, worshiped Him and kept praying, Lord, help me!

WHEN OUR DAUGHTER Dawn was a mere tyke, she was injured one day by accident. As a feisty, nonbeliever in the separation of the sexes, she was playing ball with the boys when a careless swing of the baseball bat brought forth a gash just above her eye, right at the eyebrow. The cut was not deep, but it was bloody, and we rushed her to the hospital to the accompaniment of her nonstop piercing cries.

The effect of those cries on her parents was traumatizing. The surgeon on duty responded quickly, ascertained that stitches would be called for, and seeing our apprehensive condition, invited us to step outside while the sewing took place. The crying continued unabated.

The sound of it could be heard through the door that shielded us from seeing what was happening, wrenching us inwardly, and by its intensity confirming what we already knew knowing Dawn—that the doctor had a fight on his hands.

After what seemed like an interminably long interval, the doctor emerged, holding our little treasure, now sewn up and bandaged. And with a wry spirit he said, "Well, she certainly is a female with spirit." He had discovered it, too. And so quickly.

The memory of that experience, which now is lodged securely in family oral tradition, came back to me as I was traveling the other day. This fifteenth chapter of Matthew reminds me of that incident with my daughter so many years ago. It's the unusual, even unnerving story of a female with spirit. It is also a healing story, and while it does end happily, in the sense that healing does take place and wholeness is restored, along the way some surprising, eyebrow-lifting, disturbing questions are raised. Especially the verbal picture it presents of Jesus and His apparent attitude as it's reflected in the narrative.

I wonder if we ever think about how little information we have, how few character portraits we have of women in the New Testament accounts. Lots of male figures are delineated, and delineated so clearly that even across the centuries we feel we know them well. But not too many females. The few we do have are almost limited to the writings of Luke.

Mary, of course, the mother of Jesus, appears prominently throughout the New Testament. But with that exception, we don't know even the names of many New Testament women personalities, except maybe Mary, Martha, Elizabeth, Mary Magdalene, and Anna. Lydia and Dorcas, and Priscilla and Rhoda—those are names we know, all from the Book of Acts, again, written by Luke.

The other Gospel writers tell us about Jairus's daughter, but she goes unnamed, and Simon's mother-in-law, and the widow of Nain. But they're all identified by relationship, not by name. Interesting, isn't it? Even the woman at the well about whom we do know something, that enigmatic Samaritan woman in John's Gospel, whom Jesus sent home with a whole new outlook, is unnamed.

The Bible was written by men, edited by men, preserved, and translated by men—with women's liberation still on the distant horizon.

So, it's against a background imperfectly cleansed of chauvinism that this story in Matthew stands out in sharp relief. Here is a woman, who, though still nameless, is nevertheless portrayed with enough flesh and blood, enough detail, and enough vivid imagery to come through as a real person.

She's not the wife of somebody,
 or the mother-in-law of somebody,
  or the daughter of somebody.

That is, it doesn't require a relationship with a man to establish her identity. She appears in her own right as an independent, autonomous, self-contained person, and what's more, all the evidence we have at our disposal from these verses even after being filtered through male-dominated reportage, shows her to be without question a female in spirit.

Behold authenticity at its finest. A real, live, breathing, genuine human being interacting with Jesus, in a story packed with both problems and power.

Of course, to get to the setting, you have to travel with me from where we've been before. The locale of this encounter was about as far away from home as Jesus and the disciples ever went. Galilee and Judea, where most of the Gospel events took place, are close together geographically.

The distance from Nazareth to Jerusalem was only about thirty miles. The region of Tyre and Sidon, in what is now modern Lebanon, was way up on the coast, at least one hundred miles from Jerusalem—a long way when you have to walk it, especially in sandals and robes in the heat.

What in the world was our little band of merry men doing way up there? This was foreign country, Gentile country, pagan country. The religion, the culture, and the folkways of this part of the land were totally distinct from reputable Jewish orthodoxy. What were nice Jewish boys like these doing in a place like this?

Matthew tells us Jesus had been arguing with Pharisees about religious purity, what was clean and what was unclean, what constituted appropriate association and what didn't. In the broad sense, it's the question of the company you keep. Can the righteous, the pure, and the orthodox, those who obey all the laws (or are trying to) have anything to do with those who don't meet their standards? To the Pharisees, Jesus was suspiciously lax at this point.

And now, Matthew said He and the twelve go out of the country. The Revised Standard Version Bible uses the word *withdraw*. So, they withdrew to the district of Tyre and Sidon.

Jesus the preacher, the herald of the kingdom, the proclaimer of God's reign, needed to wrestle more systematically and in greater depth with the specifics of His role in God's great plan of redemption. What about this clean/unclean business anyway? Who was clean and who wasn't? Did the Pharisees have a point, after all? Did you have to follow all the prescribed regulations to be clean, to be "right" with God?

This was the setting, I think, for the coming on stage of this remarkable Canaanite woman. Her appearance was perfectly timed to Jesus's own internal struggle. If you look closer, what a contrast between the woman here and the Pharisees' question just before. With them, the discussion centers on refinements of the faith, intricate details of the Law, and conduct.

Then immediately in the next scene, Jesus was thrown face-to-face with elemental human needs, a mother with a hurting, sick child. The woman in this story was the opposite extreme of humanity, from the point of view of the accepted Jewish orthodoxy of that day. She was a woman, first of all: strike one. Then she was a Canaanite woman, a pagan no less: strike two. And she was the mother of a child possessed by a demon: strike three. And where was her husband? She didn't have one? Oh, now we see the picture. But Jesus had seen this type before, and He had never shunned them. What's going on?

If Matthew's record of Jesus's exchange with the woman is accurate, Jesus doesn't sound like the Jesus we see in other similar situations. The Jesus who said, "Come unto me, all ye that labour and are heavy laden" (Matt. 11:28). This was so different. You can't help notice it…and feel it.

When she approached at first with her appeal, according to Matthew He didn't even answer her. Not so much a word. He was silent as stone.

She didn't go away. Instead she pleaded loudly enough to embarrass the disciples, who urged Him to send her on her way. "Do something to get rid of her. She's bothering everybody."

But He wouldn't. To the silent treatment He added explicit refusal. "I was sent only to the lost sheep of Israel. My stars. I'm sorry, you're outside my jurisdiction."

She still bored in. Throwing herself at His feet in desperation, she poured out her very soul. "Lord, help me." And then what did she get? The most chilling words of all, not only cold, but demeaning, "It is not right…to take the children's bread and throw it to the little dogs" (Matt. 15:26, AMP). *From the lips of Jesus?* Words like that? What was going on here?

Read enough commentators on this passage, and you'll be swamped with interpretations. Some say Jesus was testing the woman. Some say He was using her to teach the disciples a lesson. "See how negative and narrow you're being? See what it looks like? Shame on you."

There are those who are far more learned with the Scriptures than I even to venture a guess at what Matthew was trying to tell us. But, the more I live with this woman, the more I am struck by her tenacity, her persistence, her undiscourageable faith, the more she is illuminated.

This was a woman with spirit. Powerless and helpless before the world, the only thing she could do for the daughter she loved more than her own life was to cry out. That's all she could do. She had no influence, she had no standing, she had no prestige. All she could do was cry out, "Lord, help me." It was her only recourse and she was not going to give up on it.

This pagan woman standing at the feet of Jesus cried her heart out. Maybe we need to sit at her feet. She stood in a long honored tradition, a solid biblical tradition, even if she didn't fit the mold of somebody else's criteria. About half of the Book of Psalms is a cry for help.

Our Lord, as He hung from the cross cried out, not in a quiet resignation but in passionate fervor, "My God, my God, why hast thou forsaken me?" (Mark 15:34).

I don't know if His cry to the Father that day was in some way influenced by the cry of a Canaanite woman way up in the region of Tyre and Sidon months earlier. Maybe not. I don't know that He had the dimensions of sensitivity stretched or that He gained a greater insight into what constitutes clearness before God through that experience. But I believe the power, the passion of her plaintive cry for her child, touched Him that day. Cries can make things happen, maybe even with God.

All this woman had going for her was desperation and trust. Her cry for help got results. As the story ends, Jesus answered, "Woman, great is your faith. Let it be done for you as you wish." And her daughter was healed instantly.

chapter 22

THE POWER OF EXPECTATION

ISAIAH 2:1–5; MATTHEW 24:1–2, AMP

"Come, let us go up to the mountain of the Lord, to the house of
the God of Jacob…"

"There will not be left here one stone upon another."

"The house lights go off and the foot lights come on. Even the chattiest stop
their chattering as they wait in the darkness for the curtain to rise. In the
orchestra pit the violin bows are raised. The conductor has lifted his baton."

"In the silence of a midwinter dusk there is far off in the deep of it, somewhere
a sound so faint that for all you can tell it may be only the sound of the silence
itself. You hold your breath to listen…the extraordinary thing that is about to
happen is matched only by the extraordinary moment…just *before* it happens."[1]

EXPECTANCY. BOTH THE Isaiah passage and the Matthew passage are about
that moment. Both reflect the mood but from different perspectives. Do
they cancel each other out?

> Are they contrary?
> > Are they potentially compatible?
> > > Isaiah/Matthew,
> > > > Promise/Threat,
> > > > > Hope/Warning.

Both have to do with what is to come, yet what a difference in perspective.

Isaiah, way back seven hundred years before the birth of Jesus, had a dream,
a bold, daring dream. It was a dream about the future, about a day that ought
to be—and that could be—he thought. He wrote about it in as lovely a series of
images as you'll find in any literature:

"Come, let us go up to the mountain of the Lord, To the house of the God of Jacob; That He may teach us His ways And that we may walk in His paths." Then he added: "Nation shall not lift up sword against nation, Neither shall they learn war any more."

What a dream! In a dark and bloody time, when the whole known world was cowering before the dreaded Assyrian hordes, Isaiah envisioned an end to war forever and the dawn of an age of earthly peace. The expression of Isaiah's dream is deeply moving.

The Bible tells us of another perspective of a dream. Matthew reported that Jesus also had a dream about the future. How much was Matthew and how much was Jesus is hard to know, but what a different dream—what contrasting, conflicting images. Jesus's dream sounds like a nightmare.

They asked Him about what was to come, what lay ahead. He told them in words that even now pound on the ears with ominous intensity. The temple you see before you, He said, the very center of Jewish life and worship, will be reduced to rubble. "Not a stone will be left standing on another."

Then in words the mirror opposite of Isaiah's, He added, "Nation will rise against nation, and kingdom against kingdom, and there will be famines and earthquakes...all this is but the beginning...of the birth pangs...there will be great tribulation such as has not been seen from the beginning of the world until now. So also, when you see these signs, you may know of a surety that He is near, at the very doors. ...You must be ready, therefore, for the Son of Man is coming at an hour when you do not expect Him."

If listening to Isaiah *moves* me deeply, listening with sensitivity to the expression of the Matthew's vision *alarms* me deeply. Two sharply divergent dreams about the future: Hope and apprehension. Promise and warning. Gladness and gloom.

The juxtaposition of these two dreams is as relevant today as it was back then. We dream of a promising future, don't we? And there's evidence for it. We can look out and point to things going on in the world around us that greatly boost our confidence in what lies ahead.

But we are intelligent enough to know there are problems out there as well. We know that unemployment abounds and some no longer have jobs, some are dissatisfied with marriage or family relationships. Some of us feel trapped or dangling at the end of a rope. Some have ill parents or precarious health issues.

Maybe ol' Isaiah was just naïve. It's not all that hard to flesh out a gloomy picture, is it? This is the other side, the dark dream.

Probably most of us find ourselves somewhere between the two extremes and in our outlook combine elements of both. We see good things and we are encouraged; we see negative things that give us pause. We are both hopeful about the future and nervous at the same time. We are Isaiah one moment and Matthew the next. Regardless of how hopeful or despondent we feel as we look toward tomorrow, we tend to forget that God has a gift for us—for each of us—the present, the immediate moment...the *now*.

Take a look at Isaiah's passage again. Isaiah was confident about what was to be. He believed in it. But he didn't tell the people just to sit around and wait for it. Even as he paints his lovely picture of what is to be, he sticks in a word of command for this moment of expectancy:

"O house of Jacob, Come, let us walk In the light of the Lord."

Yes, better things are coming, a new day will dawn, but there is something you can do *in the present, in the now*, to claim that coming reality. We can walk in the light...*now*!

These passages are Advent readings, both of them. One says good things are coming; do your job *now*. The other says bad things are coming, do your job *now*. Either way, they're the same assignment.

I love fresh Georgia peaches. One day, Sara and I were heading up I-75 to Tennessee right smack dab in the middle of peach-growing season. I rolled the car window down and smelled the fragrance of those peaches for miles around. Every time we stopped for gas, we saw vendors on both sides of the road selling peaches to those traveling through—beautiful red and yellow succulent peaches.

I decided to go ahead and buy some, but Sara swore they would be cheaper on up the road. So we drove and drove and drove, looking for the best deal. "No, no, Dale. They're going to be cheaper just up ahead." Well, we drove so far that before we knew it we were out of the peach-growing section and our baskets were still empty. We had missed it.

I think ol' Isaiah and Matthew were both right regarding their dreams. If we just sit around waiting for the best to come or resign ourselves to the worst, you can miss out on a whole lot more than peaches. Right *now* we can claim the packed-down-and-running-over basket that God offers, the gift of His presence in the present, the breaking in of the timeless upon the timely, the overflowing toward the eternal into the...*now*.

I love the movie *Cat on a Hot Tin Roof*. Well, actually, I love the star actress,

Elizabeth Taylor…the young, Elizabeth Taylor. Elizabeth was about the only thing I really noticed about the movie until one day I saw a striking storyline that unfolded toward the end.

Big Daddy, played by Burl Ives in the movie, nears the end of his life with his world in shambles. He has become wealthy—lots of land, lots of material goods—but he's accomplished what he has at the expense of his family life. He has never truly loved his wife or his children in any deep sense, and thus has estranged himself from her, reduced his older son to cold detachment, and driven his younger son to alcoholism. He himself has been the show.

At the end of the movie Big Daddy discovers he has a terminal disease and soon will die. In the midst of a violent argument with his younger son, he talks of his plans for the future only to realize that he's not going to live to fulfill them. Eternal realities break in on *his present*. It hits him. How embarrassingly slow it was to come, but it finally did. He embraces his younger son, and then, for the first time in years, maybe ever, he calls his wife by her name, offers her his arm, and they take a walk together around the farm. The film ends with Big Daddy living each moment as if it were eternally significant.

It is, of course. That's the message, even in a Tennessee Williams movie. God is not only the God of the future, out there, nor only God of the past, back there. He's with us now, right here. That's what Isaiah and Matthew are trying to tell us.

Thomas Crammer's prayer says it: "…nearer to us than breathing, closer than hands and feet…"

Amos Wilder has a little poem in his book, *Grace Confounding*:

He came when He wasn't expected
As He always does,
Though a few on the night shift had
The release early.
He came when He wasn't expected
As He always does,
Though a few of the Magi were tipped off
…He is always one step ahead of us.

"The house lights go off and the footlights come on…the violin bows are raised…" *Hush!* Something is in the air. Watch! Be ready!

chapter 23

WHEN YOU ARE LONELY

MATTHEW 26:36–46

"Then saith he unto them, My soul is exceeding sorrowful,
even unto death: tarry ye here, and watch with me."

THE SAGE WOODY Allen talked about getting a letter one day delivered to his apartment mailbox in New York City. He'd been there, pining away, alone for three days without seeing another human being, and this letter came. He opened it and read it ecstatically, "I love you. I'm mad about you. I can't live without you another instant." He looked again at the envelope. It was addressed to "Occupant."

I personally feel that loneliness may be the worst of all human afflictions. The ancient Greeks thought so, anyway. Remember back in the days before Christ, when they wanted to punish someone, first they'd vote on it, by means of a little oyster shell called an "ostracod." We get our word *ostracize* from it.

And when the punishment was decided, the officials would banish him, exile him, maybe off to an island somewhere so that he was isolated, separated, cut off completely from any contact with human society. The perfect punishment they gloated—humane yet devastating. For what could be worse than eating out your heart in utter loneliness?

A lady living alone in New York City stayed up every night until after midnight listening to a certain radio station because the disk jockey had a sexy voice. When the disc jockey signed off, he always said, "Good night, especially to you."

"Try to imagine what it's like," a person from Chicago wrote recently, "to never receive a letter, never to receive a telephone call, never to have anyone ask for you. I'll tell you what it's like; it's hell, and that's the only way you can describe it."

A suicide note found on the bank of the Thames River in London said simply, "Please don't think me insane, but loneliness, at the end of each day, is like a gray ghost. And I simply can't take it any longer."

So, there you have it. Three major metropolitan cities: New York, Chicago, and London, densely populated. None of the population is immune to loneliness just because of people mass.

It's not a matter primarily of geography, though. You can be completely alone and not be lonely at all; many people are, quite happily. Some of humankind's most creative moments come about that way. And you can be absolutely surrounded by people, as in a booming city, and be the loneliest person in the world.

It's not a matter primarily of age, either. I used to think older people were the only ones who get lonely, but that's not true. No age group escapes it.

Maybe in some ways, it is harder on the elderly when you've reached that point in life where you have more friends in heaven than you have on earth, where the closest to you through the years have outrun you, where you're maybe the last one left out of a family. That's my case. I'm it.

Unfortunately for those of us who are pigeonholed in the elderly or middle-aged category, we oftentimes forget the poignant loneliness of youth. It is easy to forget after you've passed it, and some of us are no longer tuned in, but is there ever a time when you felt more alone than when you're growing up?

The loneliness of alienation,
    the loneliness of the generation chasm,
        the loneliness of trying to understand,
            the loneliness of having to face mature decisions without the tools and experience of maturity.

Of course this is a lonely thing. Maybe Anne Frank was right in her *Diary of a Young Girl*, when she wrote, "In its innermost depths, youth is lonelier than old age."

From a spiritual aspect, when you suffer from loneliness, we need to remember that Jesus Himself did, too. In all that He endured, He still needed companionship. He longed for it and yearned for it when it was taken away.

Just let your mind dwell on that scene in Gethsemane before the betrayal, where Jesus is praying for guidance and strength. I honestly think the history of the world itself was hanging in the balance here. The whole destiny of humankind is at a crossroad. Don't you know Jesus would have liked some human support, some human undergirding during that hour? Think about it. Why do you suppose He asked Peter, and James, and John to go with Him?

When they continually fell asleep, don't you know that broke His heart? That had to hurt as much as anything. They left Him, figuratively speaking, abandoned Him, so from that point on until the end He was truly alone with no other human being to share His burden.

No matter how lonely we ever get, we'll never be as lonely as Jesus was during the evening and morning preceding the Crucifixion. Because He Himself has been there, has been through this problem, we can be assured that He understands. Somehow just having that assurance makes it a little easier for me to endure.

You may not think so but there's almost always somebody else around you who is lonelier than you are, and insofar as you understand your loneliness, you may well be the most effective person in the world to meet that person's need.

I guess the only real suggestion that anyone could give someone who suffers from loneliness is that the experience of knowing God as a friend can sustain that person and see him or her through when there's nothing else they can cling to. And this is the offer of God. This invitation of God sounds like a trumpet from one end of the Bible to the other.

In Genesis 3:8–9, God walked in the garden in the cool of the evening, calling to the man He had created, "Adam, Adam, where are you?" If you remember, Abraham was called specifically the "friend of God." Isn't that a wonderful designation? God came to be with Moses there on the mountainside. Later, the Word came to Joshua: "As I was with Moses, so I will be with thee" (Josh. 1:5). And, of course, Elijah, David, and the prophets, right on down the line, picture God as coming to be with each of them. And what does the whole concept of incarnation mean? The Hebrew word is *Immanuel*, "God with us."

And when He left them in the flesh, the last recorded words He uttered were, "Lo, I am with you always, even unto the end of the world" (Matt. 28:20).

With you...with me! When you really know, when you're really grabbed by what that means, you're close to the center of what it's all about.

Two young British soldiers were lifelong friends serving in the same regiment during World War I. In the Battle of the Marne, both, side by side, went over the top to charge the enemy position. One of the two friends got back safely, but the other was shot by machine gun fire and seriously wounded.

The one who made it went to his commanding officer and asked permission to go out into no-man's-land to try to bring back his friend. "Don't be a fool," the officer said. "Go if you want to, but it's not worth it. Your friend is probably dead by now, and you'll just throw your own life away." But the soldier went anyway. Somehow he managed to find his friend, managed to drag him back through a hail of enemy fire, and somehow got back to the safety of his own line. They tumbled together into the trench bottom and lay there for a while in silence as the officer examined them.

"You see," he said finally, "I told you it wasn't worth it. Your friend is dead, and now you're wounded, too." "Oh yes, it was worth it," said the young soldier. "You see, when I got there, he was still alive, and he said to me, 'Jim, I knew you'd come.'"

This whole loneliness thing is on a scale so big the mind can't fully wrap around it. But then, isn't that the nature of the divine heart? When you are lonely, when you are hurting, when you are in trouble, when you are anything, He comes.

He's there…always… "even unto the end of the world."

chapter 24

THE NEED TO GET PAST SATURDAY

MARK 15:31, AMP

So also the chief priests…made sport of Him…saying, He rescued
others…Himself He is unable to rescue. Let the Christ (the Messiah), the King
of Israel, come down now from the cross, that we may see [it] and trust."

IT WAS JUNE of 1815 and one of the most famous battles in history was
fought in Waterloo, Belgium. The Battle of Waterloo pitted a consortium of
nations led by England… led by General Wellington, against a mighty empire,
France… led by none other than Napoleon himself.

The future of those two main belligerents hung in the balance of the battle.

Those who were in England waited breathlessly on the shore because when
the victor was determined…when the battle was decided it was already
preplanned that there would be a signal from the shores of Belgium across
the North Sea, across the English Channel, from ship to ship to shore to the
waiting eyes of those English who were anxious to see who had won.

The signal finally came. They saw the words, "Wellington Defeated," just
before a thick fog rolled in. An entire nation was devastated as the word went
from village to village. People wept bitterly. Then, the fog lifted and they were
able to see the rest of the message, "Wellington Defeated…the Enemy."

The year was approximately 33 A.D. when the largest battle of *all* history
was fought on the cross. On Saturday there was an initial word, and darkness
fell on the land. Not just physical darkness, but the most dense fog of spiritual darkness ever imagined. For that moment the initial message came, "Jesus
Christ Defeated," and that night and into the next day people walked around
in utter despair. Those who had believed in Him…those who had followed
Him…their hearts were broken. They simply could not bring themselves to get
past the horror of Saturday.

"Easter Sunday" came and brought with it the celebration of the time that the fog lifted and we could see and understand the rest of the message, "Jesus Christ Defeated...Sin and Death."

It was a cool evening in the latter part of May when John Wesley decided to take a restless stroll. The night sky was illuminated by thousands of stars in the cloudless heaven. The year was 1738. After the stroll that changed his and countless other's lives forever, he wrote, "In the evening, I went unwilling to a society in Aldersgate Street, where one was reading Luther's preface to the epistle to the Romans. About a quarter to nine, while he was deciding the change that God works in the heart through faith in Christ, I felt my heart strangely warmed. I felt I did trust in Christ, Christ alone for salvation, and an assurance was given me that He had taken away my sins, even mine, and saved me from the law of sin and death."

How do we account for what happened to John Wesley, the founder of the Methodist church, that night? Hadn't he dedicated his entire life to bringing the Word of God into the church?

Had God changed?
  Had Christ changed?

Had the power of love suddenly turned on its heels and gained new momentum? Of course not. It was Wesley's attitude that had allowed something to happen to him. The admission of need, the willingness...finally...to accept God's acceptance of him brought Wesley out of the depths. I think some people have to reach the bottom before they'll stop kicking. I know I'm still learning that.

Wesley, like most of us today, needed to get past the Saturdays. Most of us don't yet know how to live in the power of the Resurrection...in the power of that victory. That's what happened to those people at the foot of the cross, who were still living in the Saturday that came between Good Friday and Easter Sunday. Out of the depths of narrow self-reliance, comes the experience of God's all-sufficient grace.

chapter 25

IS THERE A DOCTOR IN THE HOUSE?

LUKE 1:3
"It seemed good to me also, having had perfect understanding of
all things from the very first, to write unto thee in order..."

SOMEONE HAS SAID that preachers see people at their best, lawyers see them at their worst, and doctors see them as they are.

Well, Dr. Luke saw people as they were and loved them, but more than that he knew that God loved them. He wrote about it with all the graciousness and persuasiveness he could muster.

The Gospels were each written from a particular point of view and a particular perspective. That's why we have four Gospels instead of just one, and why each one is valuable. Written by different people with different backgrounds, each one has its own distinctive flavor.

Many Christian churches have stained-glass windows symbolizing the Gospel writers. A man symbolizes the humanity of Jesus through Matthew. A lion stands for Mark and represents Jesus as the Lion of Judah whom the prophets foretold. The usual symbol of John is the eagle. John is the soaring Gospel, the philosophical Gospel.

But the traditional symbol for the Gospel of Luke is the ox, or the bull... the animal of sacrifice. There's something very meaningful, very touching, about this. Luke saw Jesus principally as the sacrifice for the whole world. There's a depth of sensitivity and feeling in this Gospel that, I don't feel, is surpassed in any other literature. Ernest Renan, a noted Christian writer in Germany, wrote, "The Gospel of Luke is the most beautiful book ever written."

What a pity we don't know more about Luke the man. I wish I did. Dr. William Barclay says that of all the writers of biblical material, Old or New Testaments, he thinks Luke would have been the one he would have liked most to know personally. He would have been a splendid dinner companion.

Luke wrote more of the New Testament than any other writer, more even than Paul. Luke/Acts originally was a single unit, and though the two books are now divided in our Bible, at first they were two chapters of a single account.

Questions still abound as to why Luke felt compelled to write, especially at about the same time that Matthew wrote. I think one reason was the need to introduce Christianity to people who didn't have a Jewish background. There was an increasing number primarily because of Paul and his remarkable success with Gentiles across the civilized world.

When we read Matthew's Gospel, it presupposes a solid grounding in the Old Testament. It presupposes a certain Jewishness. It's a book for, well, Jewish Christians. But more and more Christians weren't Jewish. They had not come into the faith by way of Judaism. Luke himself had not. The Gentiles did not have access to the Torah to know about "The Old Testament" stories. Luke is the only Gentile writer in the New Testament.

The other reason I feel Luke wrote was the desire to justify Christianity to those in power, the Romans. Twenty years earlier, under the rule of Nero, Christians were persecuted under the pretext of treason. They had a higher loyalty than to Caesar. Luke wanted to show that this new "Jesus" religion was not subversive to the state, was not intrinsically hostile toward Roman authority, that it was possible to be both a Christian and a loyal citizen. Over and over again, both in the Gospel of Luke and Acts, we see the Romans being drawn in a rather positive light. They are even praised for their open-mindedness, their fairness, and their sense of justice. Luke wanted to show his Roman readers that Christianity was not subversive; it was Nero who was distorted. Luke hoped to win public support by approving previous Roman attitudes. You could call him the church's first public relations man.

All the scholars I have read call attention to Luke as an extremely careful writer. In fact, he wrote more precisely than any other New Testament author. He wrote with something approaching the precision of a professional historian.

Luke tells us very specifically in the first chapter that his writing is based on careful investigation. Not only is that an intriguing bit of information, but it's also very important. No one denies that the Gospel of Luke is an inspired book, a God-inspired book, and yet Luke begins by saying it is the product of painstaking, meticulous research… But isn't that what inspiration is?

Not a one-sided, unilateral product,
   Not a handed-down, finished effort, but a cooperative endeavor...

God and disciple working together. How exciting the Bible becomes when we see it in that light. How great a God it takes to allow His every Word to His people to be formed that way.

The Word of God is not just bestowed from above on a silver platter. It never has been!

It's something that has to be dug out and grappled with and worked for, just as Luke tells us he did.

chapter 26

OFF TO WORK

LUKE 4:17–18, AMP

"And there was handed to Him [the roll of] the book of the prophet Isaiah.
He opened (unrolled) the book and found the place where it was written, the
Spirit of the Lord [is] upon Me, because He has anointed Me [the Anointed
One, the Messiah] to preach the good news (the Gospel) to the poor."

A T THE CENTER of the Christian faith is this man named Jesus. From day
one, Jesus was on a mission, a mission that as an adult He only had three
years to complete. So He figured He'd better get started.

As His movement gathered steam, this Jewish man came to be talked about
more and more as God, fully divine as well as fully human. Before all the big
language and grand claims, the story of Jesus was about a Jewish man, living
in a Jewish region among Jewish people, calling people back to the way of
the Jewish God. Jesus was first and foremost a Jewish rabbi and all that that
afforded Him. I'm certainly no authority, but let me try to explain to you as I
understand it.

Jesus grew up in Israel, in an orthodox Jewish region of Israel called
Galilee. Now the Jewish people who lived in Galilee believed that at a specific
moment in history, God had spoken directly to their ancestors. They believed
this happened soon after their people had been freed from slavery in Egypt and
were traveling in the wilderness south of Israel. Their tradition said that while
their ancestors were camped at the base of Mount Sinai, their leader, a man
named Moses, went up the mountain and received words from God.

They believed not only that God had spoken to Moses but also that God had
actually given Moses a copy of what He said.

They believed that the first five books of the Bible—Genesis, Exodus, Levit-
icus, Numbers, and Deuteronomy—were a copy of what God had said. They
called these five books the Torah.

They believed the best way to live was to live how the Torah said to live. And so the central passion of the people of Jesus's world was teaching, living, and obeying the Torah.

The question among the rabbis, the teachers of Jesus's day, was How young do you begin teaching the Bible, the Torah, to kids? One rabbi said, "Under the age of six we do not receive a child as a pupil; from six upwards accept him and stuff him like an ox [with the Torah]."

Education wasn't seen as a luxury or even as an option; education was the key to survival. The Torah was seen as so central to life that if you lost it, you lost everything. The first century Jewish historian Josephus said, "Above all else, we pride ourselves on the education of our children [education of Torah]."

Around the age of six, Jewish children would have gone to school for the first time. It would probably have been held in the local synagogue and taught by the local rabbi.

This first level of education, translated from Hebrew, as the "House of the Book," lasted until the student was about ten years old.

Sometimes the rabbi would take honey and place it on the students' fingers and then have them taste the honey, reminding them that God's words taste like honey on the tongue. The rabbi wanted the students to associate the words of God with the most delicious, exquisite thing they could possibly imagine.

The students would begin memorizing the Torah, and by the age of ten they would generally know it completely by heart.

The text was central to life for a Jew living in Galilee in Jesus's day. As you read the accounts of Jesus's life, notice how everybody seems to know the text. This is because from an early age Jewish people were taking in the words, and the words were becoming a part of them.

This memorization was also necessary because if you lived during that time you wouldn't have your own copy of the text. The printing press wasn't invented until fourteen hundred years later. There was a good chance you would only see the Scriptures once a week, and that was when they were brought out of the Torah ark to be read publicly.

Rabbis who taught the Torah were the most respected members of the community. They were the best of the best, they were Michael Jordan, Brett Favre, and Emmitt Smith rolled up in one. They were the smartest students who knew the text inside and out. Not everybody could be a rabbi.

By the age of ten, students had begun to sort themselves out. Some would demonstrate natural abilities with the Scriptures and distance themselves from the others. These students went on to the next level of education, which was called Bet Talmud ("House of Learning"), and lasted until sometime around the age of fourteen.

Students who didn't continue their education would continue learning the family trade. If your family made sandals or wine or were farmers, you would apprentice with your parents as you learned the family trade in anticipation of carrying it on someday and passing it down to the next generation.

Meanwhile, the best of the best, continuing their education in Bet Talmud would then memorize the rest of the Hebrew Scriptures. By age thirteen or fourteen the top students had the entire Bible memorized, beginning with Genesis and ending with Malachi.

Students in this second step of education would also study the art of questions and the oral tradition surrounding the text. For thousands of years, brilliant minds have been discussing the words of God, wrestling with what they meant and what it meant to live them out. This developed into a massive oral tradition, so as a student, you would not only be learning the text but you would also be learning who had said what in the name of whom.

Now when the rabbi would ask a student a question, he would seldom give an answer. Have you noticed how rarely Jesus answers questions, but how often He responds with another question?

Rabbis had no interest in having the student spit back information just for information's sake. They wanted to know if the student understood it, if he had wrestled with it. In the rabbinic education world, the focus was on questions, which demonstrated that the student not only understood the information but could then take the subject a step further.

When Jesus's parents found Him, He was in the temple area. He was only twelve. Notice what the text says here, "They found Him in the temple, sitting among the teachers, listening to them and asking them questions" (Luke 2:46, AMP).

Jesus later said to His disciples, "Remember, everything I learned I passed on to you."

At the age of fourteen or fifteen at the end of Bet Talmud, only the best of the best of the best were still studying. Most students by now were learning the family business. Those remaining would now apply to a well-known rabbi to become one of that rabbi's *talmidim* (disciples). The goal of a disciple wasn't just to know what the rabbi knew...but to be just like the rabbi.

This level of education was called Bet Midrash ("house of study"). A student would present himself to a well-known rabbi and say, "Rabbi, I want to become one of your disciples." When a student applied to a rabbi and said, "I want to follow you," the rabbi wanted to know a few things: Can this student do what I do? Does this student have what it takes?

After the grilling about the Torah, if the rabbi believed the student to be his worth, he would say, "Come, follow me."

The student would leave his father and mother, leave their synagogue, leave his village and his friends, and devote his life to learning how to do what his rabbi did...follow him wherever he led him. He would learn to apply the oral and written law to situations. He gave up his whole life to be just like his rabbi.

This kind of devotion is what it means to be a disciple.

One of the earliest sages of his day, Yose ben Yoezer, said to disciples, "Cover yourself with the dust of your rabbi's feet." This idea came from what everyone had seen. A rabbi would come to town, and right behind him would be this group of students, doing their best to keep up with the rabbi. By the end of the day of walking in the dirt directly behind the rabbi, the students would have the dust from his feet all over them.

So at the age of thirty, when a rabbi generally began his public teaching and training of disciples, we find Jesus walking along the Sea of Galilee.

"He saw two brothers; Simon called Peter, and his brother Andrew. They were casting a net into the lake, for they were fishermen." (See Matthew 4:18.)

Why are they fishermen? Because they aren't disciples. They weren't good enough; they didn't make the cut. This is strange, don't you think? Why do they just drop their nets when Jesus calls them to follow? Why would they quit their jobs for some rabbi they had never met?

Given the first-century context, it's clear what is going on here. Can you imagine what this must have been like—to have a *rabbi* say to you, "Come, follow me?"

Of course they would have dropped their nets. The rabbi believes you can do what he does. He thinks you can be like him.

Then Jesus came upon James and John fishing with their father. If they were still with their father and hadn't gone off and had a family of their own, we can assume that they may be around fourteen or fifteen. The point is Jesus took some boys who didn't make the cut and changed the course of human history.

We continue to read of the disciples' escapades with this Jewish rabbi they have chosen to follow. We read of Peter who, while out on the lake in a boat, saw Jesus walking on water toward them. If you are a disciple, you have committed your entire life to being like your rabbi, doing what he does.

This disciple got out on the water and he started to sink. Who does Peter lose faith in? Not Jesus; He's doing fine. Peter lost faith in himself. Peter lost faith that he could do what the rabbi did.

The entire rabbinical system was and is based on the rabbi having faith in his disciples. What frustrates Jesus to no end is that His disciples lose faith in themselves. God has an incredibly high viewpoint of His people. God believes that people are capable of amazing things.

We have been told that we need to have faith in God. What we learn more often than not is that God has faith in us. The rabbi thinks we can be like Him.

Jesus didn't call just twelve disciples.

chapter 27

THE FAITH OF ANOTHER

MARK 2:3, AMP

"Then they came, bringing a paralytic to Him, who had been
picked up and was being carried by four men."

D ON'T YOU WISH we had more details?
How old was he?
How long had he been paralyzed?
Was he brought there against his will?
We just don't know any of that. That's how the Gospel stories do you,
every time. We're given just the bare-bones outline, and the rest is left to our
imagination.

The big news of the day was about the strange carpenter fellow who had
exploded onto the scene, and nobody was quite able to pigeonhole. The coun-
tryside was buzzing about all He'd been up to.

The folks were talking about him down at the barbershop,
  and at the well…
    and over at the 7-Eleven.
      And people began to flock in…
        rich and poor, young and old.
          Crowds of people,
            pushing,
              shoving,
                elbowing,
                  shouting…trying to get to Him just to touch Him.

All day long they came, wave after wave, and the room in which He tried to
see them was continuously filled to overflowing.

Suddenly outside the house, something unusual happened. A group of men carrying a friend, a crippled man on a stretcher, tried their best to gain access to the room...no chance. Too many people. It was worse than the mall the day after Thanksgiving. They couldn't even get inside the door.

So with ingenuity born of necessity, they climbed on top of the house and with ropes, I suppose, and sheer brawn, they hoisted their friend up to the roof.

When the men reached the top, they got to work and knocked a hole in the insubstantial roofing material. So far as we know, no permission was granted; they just did it. Then, with their ropes, they lowered their buddy through the beams so that he came to rest on the floor at the feet of Jesus.

Can you just picture it in your mind? The people crowded into every corner...the crippled man suddenly the center of attention on the floor...and the friends, still on the top of the roof, looking down into the room... And Jesus, now gazing up into their faces, marveling at the confidence...no, stronger than that, *at the sheer audacity* with which they have done this nervy thing. When you really stop and think about it, it's one of the most vivid cameo shots we have in the New Testament.

And the record that it is presented to us by Mark and Luke says, "When Jesus saw *their* faith..."Get that possessive pronoun? "When Jesus saw their faith..." Not the faith of the man on the floor; the faith of the men on the roof. When Jesus saw *their* faith, He said to the paralyzed man, "Your sins are forgiven."

A man was made whole by the faith of others. The recipient was blessed, not through his own doing, but because somebody else cared enough about him and believed enough in him.

This story reminds me of the story of the turtle found sitting on the fence post. The moral, of course, is that if you're walking down the road and you see a turtle perched upon a fence post, the chances are pretty good that he didn't get there by himself.

That guy on the floor could never have done it on his own. Somebody had to bring him and put him in the location where the healing could take place, and that means somebody had to care enough to do it. It couldn't have happened otherwise.

Aren't we all, to a great extent, what we are because of the faith of others?

Aren't we all, in a large measure, what we are because somebody else along the way had, and maybe continues to have, faith and confidence in us?

We've all grown, all developed, all matured, all blossomed, all thought better of ourselves, all done better because somewhere along the line we've known that there was somebody who believed in us and we just simply didn't want to let them down. The faith of others.

We all have our stories of those who have cared enough about us to help us along the way and believe in us, and the story that comes to my mind, and I know I've shared this story with most of you before but it's just too good to pass up.

She was a Latin teacher I had in high school. I'll never forget Ms. Laird if I live to be 105.

She was undoubtedly the world's meanest woman. I'm not talking fussy or crabby or irascible. She was all of those. But *more* than those. She was just cuss-edly *mean*.

She could just look at me with those probing eyes and pick out of my brain what I didn't know. For me that was a lot. When I walked into the classroom, she had my lack of preparation catalogued. It was uncanny. She had a special eye in the back of her head. I know she did, and it peeked out through the bun. Did you ever notice how all the mean teachers wore their hair in a bun? The bun hid the third eye.

She rarely raised her voice. She didn't have to, for I have seen her with my own two eyes cut a student to ribbons from a distance of twenty paces with just a flick of her two-edged tongue.

If Ms. Laird were to walk into my office right now as I write this, I would instantly quail, turn ashen, and begin conjugating irregular verbs, and I don't even remember how to do it.

One day after a particularly grueling test over a particularly grueling campaign with Caesar in Gaul, this imperious woman cruised over to my desk, paused dramatically, and then pronounced, "Roger Dale, after school I want to see you in my office."

I knew it was not good! I entertained at that moment a rather solidly grounded suspicion that I was about to be the victim of an unmitigated disaster. If I could have chosen right then between fighting the lions in the Circus Maximus and facing the wrath of Ms. Laird in her den, I would have overwhelmingly chosen the former.

I prayed, I sweated…as an act of atonement, I even threw away the copy of *Lady Chatterly's Lover* I had hidden in my locker—everything I could think of.

But when the appointed hour came, I was there, because I knew better than not to be. She received me coldly, positioned me in a chair, and then closed the door behind me—thus ending all possibility of escape.

Drawing herself up to her full five feet one-and-a-half inches, Mrs. Laird clenched her jaws, closed one eye and sort of squinted out of the other one...*then brandished a test paper in my face!* All I could see was my name and a rampaging horde of red X marks.

"This," she hissed, "is the worst test paper I have ever seen in my life. How do you expect to get into college with grades like these?"

College? I thought. College? Are you out of your tree? What are you talking about? I am not worried about college, Lady; just let me out of the tenth grade. If I can just get out of this office, I'm gone...I promise. I'm out of here. I'll never set foot in this county again.

These were internal expressions, you understand. I didn't say anything. I just sat there and she continued. As she talked, I began to get the shock of my life. Something was happening to Ms. Laird. I looked up in utter stupefaction and saw a change.

Those hard lines around her mouth were softening. She wasn't exactly smiling; I knew she couldn't smile. There was something there I had never seen before: a touch of friendliness, even tenderness in her eyes. Finally, in the softest voice I had ever heard her use, she said, "Oh, Dale, for your own sake, don't waste your talent. You can do so much better work than this."

If I hadn't been a big sophomore, I think I would have cried. *That was Ms. Laird talking to me like that...* Ms. Laird, the evil spirited woman.

She was actually concerned about me. She thought I had some promise. She believed in me. She expected better of me than I had been producing and that got to me.

Something happens to you when you know somebody believes in you and is counting on you.

Let's lift it to an even higher dimension...*the gospel God Himself believes in you.* The proof is in the incarnation.

The gospel is that He has come to us, believed in us enough to bring us, crippled and paralyzed though we are, to the place of total healing. *The faith of another* has made us whole.

The miracle of it is that now we can believe in ourselves; now we are free to respond, because God Himself thinks we are worth something.

Wallace Hamilton, in one of his books, tells of a play called *Green Pastures* by Marc Connelly. The highlight of the play concerns the Old Testament prophet Hosea. God in His anger has refused to have anything more to do with his faithless children who have forgotten Him and are now in bondage for their sins.

Three old patriarchs—Abraham, Isaac, and Jacob—come into God's office in the sky to play poker with Him. As they sit around His desk playing five-card draw, they beg Him to have mercy on His people and deliver them.

God has made up His mind. He's seen how the people have been living. He's seen their contentiousness and their sin. He's washed His hands on them forever.

Then He notices something. He keeps seeing the shadow of a man on His door...a man walking back and forth outside, deliberately casting his shadow against the door of heaven.

God says, "Who is that, anyway?" The patriarchs tell him it's Hosea, the sensitive Old Testament prophet who loved a woman who went bad, left him, and became a prostitute. But he loved her anyway. He kept loving her, and finally he went out into the pigpen where her life of degeneration had taken her...and brought her back home, forgave her, and gave her another chance.

For a long time God stands at the window, looking down listening to the noise and cries of the people in their bondage and remembering the unquestionable love displayed by Hosea to his wife Gomer. He finally can stand it no longer. Gabriel hands Him His hat, top coat and cane, and He descends the stairway of heaven with a baby in His arms to give His children one more chance. Jesus Christ has come to Earth.

It was for you and me that He came on one cold wintry morning because we matter to Him... We are important to Him and He believes in us...*the faith of another.*

chapter 28

THE FORGIVEN WOMAN

LUKE 7:44, AMP

"Simon, Do you see this woman?"

I'M SURE HE squirmed as He talked to him about values, priorities, and about...*her*.

He squirmed until he was ashamed.
Squirmed until he knew he had to change.
Squirmed until he realized the full extent of his phoniness.

He was outclassed by the tears, the hair, the perfume box, and the honesty of a woman who was a common sinner.

I'd like to tell the story from the vantage point of the two men, Jesus and Simon, as this *woman* steps into the home of Simon.

"Simon, do you see this woman?"

"My stars, what do You mean, do I see her? You've got to be kidding. Why, of course I see her." Simon saw her the way a sniper sees an enemy's uniform. Certainly he saw her. Wasn't he the host? Wasn't this his home? Hadn't he sent out all the invitations? And this...*woman*...came crashing into his home and blew the whole thing wide open.

Now Simon had to tell all those around that he did know her. "I know you, woman. I recognize you. I know your kind. I've seen you out there in the streets with your painted face and cheap perfume. You don't fool me for one minute with that act of pious contribution. What a fraud. I know who you really are."

"What bothers me, though, is why Jesus doesn't know her. What's the matter with *Him*? Is He blind? Am I all wrong about Him? I thought He had insight...

I thought He had intuition...

I thought He knew people... He seemed so special. But, now look at Him,

119

practically fawning over her. This man, if He were a prophet, would have known who and what manner of woman this is that touches Him. She's a sinner."

"Simon, do you see this woman?" Isn't it astounding with what economy the Gospel told these stories? So compact and jammed with meaning...so much was conveyed, so simply, both by what was said, and, quite often by what was not.

"You need to understand, Simon. You need to understand that a grosser sinner may be nearer to forgiveness than you. You need to understand that fellowship with God isn't just a question of who is least sinful, but who is most patient...and most often open to receive His grace.

"Do you see this woman, Simon? Look again. You see the outside, but is that all there is?

You see the mask...the front...the exterior... the make-up... the plastic... the conduct...the performance. Do you see nothing more?

Do you not see her grief, her shame, the agonizing of her heart?

"Simon, your religion is contrived and artificial. You do all the right things for all the wrong reasons. Religion isn't something you use, Simon—it's the other way around. When it's real, it's something that uses *you*! That catches hold of you. That grabs you and wrenches your very insides.

"Of course, Simon, she's a sinner. Don't you think I know that? But, she's an acknowledged sinner. She knows it; we all know it. But, that's not the point. Look at what sin has done to her...that's the point. It's broken her, Simon, as yours never has. Those are real tears, and they come from deep within.

"Look at her real close, Simon. What an outpouring of affection. So generous, and warm, and wasteful, and extravagant...the way love is always expressed when it's authentic.

"Don't you know why she's acting the way she is right now, Simon?" *Because she's been forgiven.* Something has come into her life, something that wasn't there before. She's come to experience love without a hook in it. *And now she's reacting the only way genuine love can express itself,* by wanting to reciprocate.

"There's a cross in her love, Simon. There's not one in yours, not a splinter, not a nail, not so much as a broken piece of bark. Simon, you love as a favor *to* Me; she loves because of a favor *from* Me that turns the whole thing inside out.

"Your love comes from the will; hers from the heart. You love because you decide to; she because she can't help it. You love to show off your loveableness; she loves because of forgiveness.

"In a few moments I'm going to say to her, 'Depart in peace,' and let her go out to begin all over with a clean slate, without the drag of the past. I know what she's done to your protocol.

"When I came into your house, you gave Me no kiss, no water, no oil, not even for my head. She's been washing my feet with expensive oil since she came in. From her tears, from her gratitude, from her hair, from that lavish oil that used to be used for sin, I want you to learn about the extravagance of love, Simon.

"I know what you're thinking, Simon. *If He were a prophet, He'd see through this woman.* Well, Simon, I see through her all right, but most importantly, I see through you!"

I'll step out of character now. I hope I haven't taken too many liberties here or taken the story too far out of context. It just seems to me that in this passage we have a little man who thinks he knows so much being questioned by a *real* man who does. Can't you just close your eyes and see our Lord maybe putting His hand on Simon's shoulder, looking at him intently—not with eyes of an avenging eagle, not with hate or rejection, but the gentle, penetrating eyes of the Lamb of God.

I don't know the outcome like many stories told in the Bible, but I'd like to think that Simon saw that woman as she was leaving his house—really saw her for the first time, not as a thing anymore, not as an object, or a stereotype, but as a person. And I would like to think that even after that experience, if on a night when he couldn't sleep because of the rumbling of conscience, the gnawing away of his pride and self-righteousness, that he would remember all over again that special evening with the Lord. And through the darkness, the gentle, insistent voice of Jesus calling him by name: "Simon, do you see?"

chapter 29

RICH MAN, POOR MAN

LUKE 16:19

"There was a certain rich man, which was clothed in purple and fine linen, and fared sumptuously every day: and there was a certain beggar named Lazarus."

IT'S A TROUBLING story—frankly, a disconcerting story, as many of His stories are. It stings, it bites, even across the centuries. It goes for the jugular.

If it weren't so simple and direct—maybe that's the problem—if it weren't so transparent and uncomplicated, we could perhaps deal with it better. It's a contrast of two lives of two deaths the contrast of two eternities.

I'm not certain if the story is an actual historical incident or if it's pure parable. But if it is, it's the only one Jesus told where one of the characters is named. He doesn't do that anywhere else.

Two characters: "There was a certain rich man, which was clothed in purple and fine linen, and faired sumptuously every day" (Luke 16:19).

Do you realize that's the only description we have of the man? That's actually all we know about him. Tradition has named him *Dives*, but you don't find that in the Bible. *Dives* is simply the Latin word for "rich man." Jerome called him that in the fourteenth century when he wrote his Vulgate Edition of the Bible. The name has stuck ever since.

Now it's no disgrace in the Bible to be rich. It's no disgrace today. The Bible doesn't disparage having money. Abraham himself was a very wealthy man.

It's no sin to be rich, and yet it *is* sad. It's sad if the *only* thing, if the *only* definitive statement you can make about a person is to say that he's rich. That becomes a different matter. It's not immoral, exactly; It's not illegal to be rich. But if that's all you can honestly say, it's certainly terribly thin.

Can you picture him, though? Can you recognize him? I think if I were to speculate, I would see a man who slowly became what he became...not overnight, but over time.

No doubt there was ability, probably *nobility*. He grew, expanded, bought some franchises, sold those to someone in the Midast...made a bundle. But then, something changed him, something down inside. His success thwarted his decency. The very achievement of some of his goals eroded his values.

Means became ends,
   goods became goals,
      clients became things,
         things became treasures.

The larger the inventory, the larger the alarm system...because every day there were more wolves and more Lazaruses at the door.

Finally he locked the door and pulled the shades. Only Dives and Mammon were left in the house and, as C.S. Lewis put it, "Mammon had the larger appetite."

I seriously doubt if Dives ever honestly did see Lazarus...as a human being. It would have been too painful. But the older he became, the harder he had to run, the more he had to frolic, the more coconut he had to have in his ambrosia, the tighter around himself he had to pull the shades of protective security.

There's no description in the account of Lazarus's character, either. Only the outcome in the epilogue gives us the essential element.

Being utterly destitute could have driven him to desperation...or worse. It would be a travesty to say that Lazarus had plenty of time out there to cultivate his spiritual life, but only someone with a full belly would have the gall even to suggest it.

Not because of his poverty, but in spite of it, in spite of the sores, and driving rain, and gnawing hunger...in spite of the coldness of Dives's insulation, Lazarus trusted God. And that's the bottom line. The name Lazarus literally means "God is my helper." Though he had nothing, even less than nothing, Lazarus never abandoned faith in the eternal goodness.

And when you boil it all down, that's the real difference between the two men. The one shut his hand tightly around "things" and squeezed them without regard for anyone else; the other opened his hand in simple gratitude and gave thanks for everything he received.

The tragedy in Dives's life is not that he was horrendous, but that in spite of his bounty he allowed himself to become heartless. Not even misfortune made Lazarus bitter; not even blessings made Dives sensitive.

I have seen this story played out each time I travel to Central America as a representative in faith of my church. I see people who, compared to the wealth that I leave behind in Winter Park, don't have the right to be happy. They don't even have a cement floor to walk on in their homes or a window to shut out the night air. They don't have electricity or running water other than the stream down the road. But what I do see and feel and share is the deep, abiding love that these people have in their Lord. And you can see this love through the eyes of their children. You can't fake that kind of love, nor can you buy it with "things." And they sing it out as loud and as long as they can, without the aid of a spiffy embossed hymnal. They know the words by heart because that's where the words are coming from the heart.

Yes, I have seen this story played out and I continually return, admittedly, for selfish reasons. I want what they have!

It would almost seem that whenever God blesses us lavishly, he puts a Lazarus at the back door to remind us that the only wealth that lasts, the only wealth than *can* last, is the wealth that's used to bless.

This parable played a role in the life of Albert Schweitzer. In his biography, he claims it was this story more than any other that convinced him to become a missionary. He read it, and it grabbed him. He read it over and over; he studied it and wrestled with it and finally came to the conclusion that for him, the continent of Africa was Lazarus, lying wretched and hungry at the back door of wealthy Europe.

Two people, two deaths, two eternities. Choice hardens into habits, habit produces character, and character lasts even into eternity.

chapter 30

PRAYER PERSPECTIVES

LUKE 18:9–14

"Two men went up into the temple to pray; the one
a Pharisee, and the other a publican."

FIRST-CENTURY PALESTINE... eastern end of the Mediterranean... Roman
occupied territory...

Society, highly structured and tense. In any comparison between a Pharisee
and a publican in Jesus's day, it was inevitably the Pharisee who came out on
top.

The Pharisee was far from being a bad guy, at least in public opinion.

A Pharisee was the epitome, the embodiment, the paradigm of moral
rectitude.

On the other hand, a publican was the quintessential villain. A publican
was a tax collector. There was nothing lower in the minds of the people than a
publican. A publican was a tax collector.

The Pharisee was the honorable one in society; the publican was a scumbag.
And yet, look who gets the accolade.

It's precisely that twist, the unexpected reversal of accented wisdom that gives
the story its punch. Let's step a little closer to this man, the Pharisee... especially *this* Pharisee.

He was a man who was dead earnest about his service to God. He didn't play
around with it. It was not something secondary or peripheral to him. He took
his religion seriously. We are told in the reading that he tithed. The heart of the
matter is usually revealed when it touches either the stomach or wallet.

A church member said to his preacher one day, "Preacher, everybody in this
church gives until it hurts. It's just that some of us are more sensitive to pain
than others."

Well, that's not how it was with this man. Not only did he tithe, but he also sacrificed and fasted. His obligation to God was just as real to him as the coins that jingled in his pocket.

The publican was a tough-minded old coot...from the outside, at least. Here's a weather-beaten, streetwise opportunist in a position with no balances to check him, to make a killing at the expense of his fellow countrymen.

Publicans were Roman appointees; they were company men. The Romans didn't care how much extra they gouged from the people, how much beyond the limit they charged, as long as they turned in their quota. Publicans were traitors who fleeced their own people to line their own pockets.

So, on the ethical level, here we have it:
the man with integrity...the man without scruples;
the man of impeccable morals...the man of shady morals;
the man who would do nothing out of line...the man who would do anything he
could get away with;
the man who builds up...the man who tears down;
the man of respect...the man of disrepute.

In this story, Jesus condemned this one and praised that one? Maybe there's something we're overlooking here. Apparently what God sees when He looks at a person, and what people see are not always the same.

Jesus's approval of the publican and his disapproval of the Pharisee weren't based on their deeds at all. God's acceptance or rejection doesn't depend on what we do, on our record of loving and charitable actions, or on the lack of them. It depends simply on His *grace*, totally apart from moral worthiness, and on whether we are willing to accept it—on His terms. "By grace we are saved through faith."

I have heard that in some of the more extreme forms of fundamental Islam, on the day of judgment, the Muslim believer will appear before Allah dressed only in his nakedness—except around his neck there will hang a slate, divided in half.

On the one half, a mark for every evil or wicked deed performed in life will appear, and on the other half, a mark for every good or thoughtful deed will appear. If there are more of the former, the person will be plunged immediately into eternal punishment. If there are more of the latter, the person will immediately enter eternal paradise. *It's as simple as that.*

Not so in Christianity. Deeds alone don't determine destiny. *God looks on the inside* to the attitude. The best deeds come out of the best faith, and it's faith that's paramount.

And here we see the point so graphically reflected in the attitude of two men at prayer in the temple:—*one* with a strong A in conduct, but with a spirit of self-congratulation about it; the *other* with an absolute F in conduct—a flunking grade there—but with a spirit of heartfelt repentance.

Looking at these two men whose actions are so different, whose lifestyles are so far apart, and whose approaches to God in prayer are so divergent, I guess the thing that shakes me up the most is that I see something of myself in both of them.

Sometimes, we're just like the Pharisee...doing the right things, good things, maybe even occasionally noble things, and yet doing them for questionable reasons.

Sometimes we're just like the publican, doing unscrupulous things, and feeling terrible about it.

You know what the beautiful truth of the publican's experience is? He knew he didn't have a leg to stand on before God, but he admitted it. He confessed it through prayer. That's the *key*: No sham, no pretence, no cover-up. He was what he was and he said so.

I know these two men...know them only too well. In the light of God's scrutiny, our best efforts are unworthy, but in the light of God's love, our worst fears are unfounded.

"Two men went up to the temple to pray." If only the Pharisee had kept his eyes shut and looked only at God instead of around to compare himself with another human being, especially one whose heart he couldn't see, he might not have been so cocky. He would have been chastened, but he would have been closer to home.

chapter 31

THE NEED FOR MEANING

Luke 18:18–19; Mark 10:17–30; Matt. 19:16–30
"And a certain ruler asked Him, Good Teacher...what
shall I do to inherit eternal life?"

Do you know what I think that guy was really looking for, that young man who assaulted Jesus on the street beseeching help?

It's a great story, an unforgettable story...one that just reaches down into your very soul and tears your heart out. One of the most vivid the Bible tells. We even have a name for it: "The rich young ruler."

He ran, he kneeled, he implored, "Good Master, what must I do to have eternal life?"

Do you know what I think he was really looking for? Meaning. Some kind of rationale. He was looking for help in finding some meaning in his life.

This guy was frantic. He had to have an answer. There was something missing, a vacuum at the center. He was running off in all directions at once, desperately trying to "put it all together" so he could cope.

I think the last thing in the world he was concerned about was an academic discussion. He was a young man, and young men think they'll live forever.

He wasn't even consciously thinking about theological issues at all...*he wanted help. He wanted practical, sensible help in hammering out a purpose in life.*

"What must I do?" You can almost hear his voice crack. "*What must I do to have eternal life?*"

Now, *eternal* in the biblical sense is never just a quantitative word. It always has qualitative overtones. Eternal life, in New Testament terms, is always more than just, unending, relentless, inexorable, ongoing continuation...that sounds sort of "hellish," if you really think about it.

New Testament eternal life is rich, full, abundant life, overflowing, zestful life. It's a life that matters, a life that counts for something, a life that when you wake up in the morning, you're ready to hit it. "How can I find that?" he was asking.

"I don't have it now, and it's obvious by your demeanor, sir, that you not only have it, but you know how to give it away.

Help me. Please! I want to live, I want my life to have significance, I want it to have meaning. *What must I do to have eternal life?*"

Who is this young man, anyway? Why does he look so familiar? Don't you recognize him? I think I finally know who he is. Paste my name on the front instead of "rich young ruler," and I think I come pretty close to identifying this guy.

Call him the personification of contemporary man or woman. Call him just another striking example of the timeless relevance of this remarkable old book.

I think this nameless, faceless, rich young man's personal quest symbolizes the thing nearly every one of us would like to be able to clutch more tightly and hold on to more securely—a deeper sense of *meaning*.

Like this rich young ruler, we have everything except the spark to make it mean something.

> We can **do**, but we don't know **why**.
> We can **go**, but we don't know **where**.
> We can **give** but we don't know **how**.
> We can **accomplish** but we don't know **what**.
> We have enormous ability...what we lack is *aim*.
> We have enormous power...what we lack is *purpose*.
> We have all kinds of means...what we lack is the
> *meaning*.

And so we, too, become frantic. We run and hide; we knock ourselves out trying to entertain ourselves. "We eat greedily the husks of trivial, time-consuming amusements and then wonder why we don't get any nourishment" (Author unknown).

George Hunter told the story of "Tex" Evans, a Methodist layman who was a real character. Some called him the Will Rogers of the United Methodist Church. He could be entertaining, but he knew where he was coming from.

Once Tex Evans was invited to preach at a small chapel during the Baltimore Annual Conference. When he arrived at the little church, some men from the congregation were standing outside, visiting together. Tex listened as the men told him about the historical significance of a river just a few yards away. Bishop Francis Asbury had once crossed that river during a flood just so he could keep a preaching appointment.

"Do you want us to tell you how Francis Asbury came across the river?" the men asked Tex Evans.

"Nah," he said, "I don't care nothin' about that. I don't want to know *how* he came across. I want you to tell me *why* he came across."

That's the point. That's the "rest of the story." If the motivation, the purpose, the meaning is there, then the rest falls into place. But it hadn't yet for this young man, and maybe it hasn't yet for some of the rest of us. "Good Master, what must I do to have eternal life?"

Look closely at the *verbs in this story*. Go, sell, give, come, follow.

Oh, I know that's oversimplifying it. I know the implications would be staggering if everybody did what *this* man was told to do. One shudders to think what it might mean for banks, credit unions, and my own personal checking account. *But the principle is clear.*

In Jesus's answer there is a fundamental approach to life that, if followed rigorously, is guaranteed to produce meaning, the thing all of us are looking for.

Meaning comes precisely when you quit grubbing after it and begin losing yourself in matters that are bigger than you are. That's what Jesus was trying to say to the young man. Go, sell, give, come, follow.

All these verbs have to do with dethronement. They have to do with committing yourself as opposed to grasping for yourself. They have to do with getting yourself out of the center, so that something larger and more enduring can come in and take its rightful place there.

When E. Stanley Jones was a missionary in India, he was asked once by the church to assume an additional special assignment over and above the already back-breaking load he was carrying. He accepted the assignment and prepared himself for it, not by cutting down somewhere else, but by spending an extra hour in prayer, getting up one hour earlier.

True meaning comes most fully when you give yourself, genuinely give yourself, to the worship of a God who is bigger than you are.

When you finally let God do what He wants with you...

When you finally stop insisting that *you* have to be the one to decide the agenda and the program...

When you finally let *Him* be God in your life, *meaning finally emerges.*

Dr. Viktor Frankl, a German Jewish psychiatrist, was shipped to Auschwitz, Hitler's death camp. Experiencing all the atrocities that Auschwitz offered, Dr. Frankl said at the end, "A person who has a *why* for living can put up with almost any *how.*"

In the final analysis, meaning isn't something you fashion; it's more something that grasps *you.*

"What must I do to have eternal life?"

Go...sell...give...come...follow...and nothing can separate us from His love.

chapter 32

THE GOOD NEWS OF HUMBLENESS

LUKE 19:28–40; PHIL. 2:5–11, AMP

"Go into the village yonder; there, as you go in, you will find a donkey's colt tied, on which no man has ever yet sat. Loose it and bring [it here]."

FOR SOME REASON, I keep coming back to that donkey, that little humble beast of burden that carried Jesus into town that day. At the center of the parade that marked His entrance into Jerusalem for the final week of His life, and at the center of worship two thousand years later on the day we call Palm Sunday, is that little donkey.

> Palm Sunday. It's just around the corner, just over that hill.
>> Is it a happy day or a sad day?
>>> Is it a day of shouting, or a day of weeping?
>>>> Do we blow kazoos, or do we need hankies?
>>>>> The mood of Easter is clear cut and sharply drawn.

But out of nowhere pops Palm Sunday. It breaks into that dark, ominous mood. You aren't looking for it, you aren't expecting it it just all at once pierces the cloud like a ray of light. And coming when it does, and where it does, just five days before the Crucifixion, and after six weeks of Lenten preparation, it has a jarring, discordant effect. Evangelist David Ring calls it, "Coronation just before collapse."

In Luke's version, you sense undercurrent, you sense mystery, shadows, growing tension. He says nothing about crowds at all—no throngs, no great multitudes. There are no hosannas, no branches cut from trees. If we had only Luke's account, we wouldn't even call it Palm Sunday. We'd call it Garment Sunday, I suppose or Old Clothes Sunday. There's no mention of palm branches anywhere.

Even more, author Fred Craddock reminds us, it's very much a disciple event.

Who places Jesus on the donkey? *The disciples.*

Who spreads garments on the road? *The disciples.*

Who rejoices and praises God? *Same answer.* It's exclusively an "in-house" affair.

I heard somebody say in a sermon one time that Palm Sunday was probably the single happiest day in Jesus's life. I liked the sermon but the more I've thought about it, the less I'm inclined to agree. (You're permitted to disagree with a minister every now and then.) Given the context, how could it be? Do we think for a minute he was fooled by what was going on? Do we think He was taken in by the glitter and hoopla?

The church calls it the Triumphal Entry, but it's really triumphant only in the light of the subsequent development. It's Easter that makes Palm Sunday look good, not vice versa. Palm Sunday makes no sense apart from Easter. In fact, far from being triumphant at the time, His entry into the city really only hastened the tightening of the net around Him. It was already in place, and already closing; this only sped up the process.

Riding in as Jesus did, challenging the authorities as He did, with such brazenness, almost guaranteed a ferocious reaction. It was a challenge they had to answer. In poker terms, He not only called them, but He raised the ante. Of course, they had to do something. Just five frantic days, and it was over, or so they thought.

There are two images from the two passages that help me to understand this Palm Sunday story a little better. They're both authentic and complementary. One is a visual image; the other is a verbal one. One addresses the eye, the other the ear, but both convey a common emphasis so characteristic of Jesus.

In Philippians 2:8, Paul wrote, "And being in human form, He humbled himself, and became obedient unto death, even death on a Cross." He humbled Himself—that's the verbal image. And the visual image, from the Gospel story, is that pitiful, little donkey.

Luke was explicit. The donkey wasn't even mature; it was a colt.

Can you imagine how others might have come to town? Pontius Pilate, the Roman governor, would have ridden in a chariot pulled by pure white, magnificent stallions festooned with the plumage of imperial authority. *Jesus entered the city on the back of a little donkey, and a borrowed one at that.*

A political leader like Herod Antipas would have been surrounded by security guards—armed men, paid men—who would have held back the crowd from pressing too close, to protect their man from possible harm.

Jesus was surrounded by His friends and followers from many walks of life, and He rode into the midst of the people, almost at their height.

A military leader, in the style of Annas or Caiaphas, would have moved pompously through the crowd, garbed in bright priestly robes, hedged in by an orderly contingency of other minions who would have prevented him from even being touched by anyone unclean. *Jesus dressed in His usual attire, nothing fancy or ornate, and simply plodded along humbly, not shrinking from the touch of anyone.*

The truly humble person rarely thinks of humility. Kagawa, the great Japanese Christian who in the early years of the twentieth century worked so hard and long in the slums of Japan, once came to the United States to make a speech at a conference. The time came for his presentation, but Kagawa wasn't there. They looked around for him, couldn't find him, then finally located him in the men's room of the conference hall. He was picking up paper towels that the delegates had tossed away and thrown to the floor. He said, "I didn't want the workers to have extra, unnecessary work imposed on them because of the carelessness of my fellow Christians."

God long ago decided how He would go about winning back His estranged and lost creation. Maybe He considered doing it by coercion. Maybe at times He was tempted to adopt the sledgehammer or the dynamite approach. But, thank God, He decided not to use that kind of power. He decided He would win people back one by one, one at a time, not through power from without, but through lures from within, not by coercion, but by persuasion, not by playing on our fears, but by tugging on our hearts. How perfectly Jesus reflects that.

Riding into town on a donkey is made from the same cloth as being born in a manger, and working in a carpenter shop, and eating with publicans and associating with lepers and hobnobbing with sinners and not worrying today about what may or may not happen tomorrow and "being obedient unto death, even death on a cross."

chapter 33

PREPARING FOR THE PARADOX

JOHN 1:6

"There was a man sent from God, whose name was John."

CAN YOU SEE him? He's right there in the front lobe of your imagination; unlike many of the other members of the cast he stands out so clearly. It's hard to picture John the Gospel writer or the Samaritan woman or Nicodemus or Mary Magdalene—or Jesus Himself, perhaps—in His case, because His very complexity can be imagined in so many ways.

But John the Baptizer...who can't visualize him? Big, raw-boned, vigorous, young...still young when he died.

There was the ugly business between King Herod Antipas and his step-daughter, Salome. She demanded John's head on a platter because he called her mother, Herodias, what she really was, and let me tell you, it wasn't pretty. It didn't sit very well, to say the least, and Salome got her revenge.

John was probably about thirty years old when it happened...He couldn't have been much older since we know he was just six months older than Jesus. He was a young man in his prime.

Robust, healthy, muscular, with a cast-iron stomach. (How long would yours last on a diet of honey and locusts?)

I suspect he had a beard and a really good suntan. And there would be the aroma.

His attire, desert chic, was a tunic made of camel's hair, accented with a leather girdle around the waist, and topped off with leather sandals. Tie it all together with an urgent tone of voice; a sharp, cutting message; eyes that could absolutely burn a hole through hypocrisy; and you've got yourself a force to reckon with.

This is the man all the Gospel writers use to begin their account of the life of Jesus.

All four of them point to John as the forerunner,
  the stage-setter,
    the preparer for the beginning of Jesus's redemptive ministry.
    He was not the good news but the trumpeter of the
      imminence of the Good News.
      He was not the kingdom but the herald of the kingdom
      and the announcer of what's to come.

John saw it clearly and proclaimed it. He was the essence of the Old Testament story...an accusing index finger pointing with a glare in his eyes. God was getting His people ready through centuries of chastening and molding in preparation for the great breakthrough.

I believe...if we look, we can see that John is to Jesus what the Old Testament is to the New...what law is to the gospel, what promise is to fulfillment.

I can hear John saying to the people, "Look, this Christmas thing, this incarnation thing, this Jesus business is something God has been working on all along, right under our noses.

We didn't see it, we didn't understand what was going on. Until just now we had no idea this is what God was planning for His world His hurting, suffering creation.

But all along, He had redemption on His mind, and He was sending out messengers to lay the groundwork, to prepare the way of the Lord."

John was a man of the people. He saw the human condition, saw the sense of estrangement between the human heart and God's heart. He often spoke of that condition. He called it by its name, its proper name—sin. With untrembling boldness, he never left them without hope that by turning back to God there could be reconciliation.

John's message is still pertinent to each one of us today. For we have all sinned and need to be cleansed. His message is not the last word of deliverance...

It's not the last step...but it is the first step. His call to repentance has not been replaced. God, in His Son, has graciously responded.

"After me comes one mightier than I, the thongs of whose sandals I am not worthy to stoop down and untie." (John 1:26, 27)

One who has been in the limelight and received the plaudits of the crowd often finds it hard to see the mantle of approbation passed on to someone else. Ability and humility don't often sleep together.

Maybe his true greatness and the reason Jesus said, "Among those born of women there has risen none greater than John the Baptist," was John's selflessness, which is, after all, the very embodiment of being a Christian.

chapter 34

DON'T BE AFRAID, JUST BELIEVE

JOHN 11:40, AMP

"Jesus said to her, Did I not tell you and promise you that if
you would believe...you would see the glory of God?"

T HE WORLD SAYS, "Seeing is believing." God says, "Believing is seeing."
Faith always precedes understanding in spiritual matters. Faith means
knowing that something is real, even if we do not see it.

There is a touching story about a message found on the wall of a concentration camp during World War I. On the wall, a prisoner had carved these words:

I believe in the sun, even though it does not shine.
I believe in love, even when it is not shown.
I believe in God, even when He does not speak.

I try to imagine the person who etched those words so many years ago. I
try to envision his or her skeletal hand gripping the broken glass or stone that
cut into the wall. I try to imagine his eyes squinting through the darkness as
he carved each letter. What hand could have cut such a conviction? What eyes
could have seen good in such horror?

Larry, father of two little girls, Alice and Jo Anne, enjoyed teaching them
the mysteries of life by playing childhood games with them. One evening, he
asked eight-year-old Alice to go through the den while he instructed the six-
year-old Jo Anne to stand on the other side of the room and verbally guide her
safely across the room.

With phrases like, "Take two baby steps to the left," and "Take four giant
steps straight forward," Alice successfully navigated her sister through a treach-
erous maze of chairs, a vacuum cleaner, and a laundry basket.

Then it came Jo Anne's turn to be the navigator. She guided Alice past her
mom's favorite lamp and shouted just in time to keep her from colliding with

the wall when she thought her right foot was her left foot. After several treks through the darkness, the game stopped, and they discussed how each felt about being guided through what seemed like total darkness and the unknown.

"I didn't like it," Jo Anne said. "It's scary going where you can't see."

I was afraid I was going to fall over something or bump into something," Alice agreed. "I kept taking little steps just in order to be safe."

I believe many grown-ups can relate to this story. We don't like the darkness and the unknown either. But we walk in it. Of course we complain about how scary it is to walk where we can't see. We've reason to be cautious; for we are blind. We cannot see the future. We have absolutely no vision beyond the present.

We are all Alice and Jo Anne with their eyes shut, groping through a dark room, listening for a familiar voice…but with one difference. Their surroundings are familiar and friendly. Ours can be hostile and quite possibly life changing. Our decisions can affect not only our lives, but also those around us. Try as we might to walk as straight as we can, chances are a toe is going to be stubbed, and we are going to be hurt.

Jairus was a man who tried to walk a straight line. As you recall, Jairus was the leader of the synagogue. In the days of Christ, the leader of the synagogue was the most important man in the community. The synagogue was the center of religion, education, and social activity. It was like being the highest-ranking professor, the mayor, and the best NBA player all in one.

Jairus had it all. Who could ask for more? Yet Jairus did. He *had* to ask for more. I bet he would have traded everything for just one assurance that his daughter would live.

There are times in life when everything we have to offer is nothing compared to what we are asking to receive. Many of us know that personally. What could a man offer in exchange for his child's life? There are no games, no masquerades. Jairus was blind to the future, but he believed Jesus knew the future.

Jesus turned to Jairus and pleaded, "Don't be afraid, just believe." Jesus compelled Jairus to see the unseen. Jesus implores all of us to not limit our possibilities to the visible. Don't always listen to the audible. Believe there is more to life than what we have been surrounded by all these years. Either live by the facts or walk by faith. The choice is ours.

Well, maybe, just maybe, we can learn something from Alice and Jo Anne. After they had each taken their turns guiding each other through the house, their father decided to add a diabolical twist. On the last trip, he snuck up behind Jo Anne, who was walking around with her eyes shut, and he whispered, "Don't listen to her. Listen to me. I'll take care of you."

Jo Anne stopped. She analyzed the situation and made her choice between the two voices. "Be quiet, Daddy," she giggled and then continued in Alice's direction. The father then grabbed the lid of a pan and began banging it with a spoon. Jo Anne jumped and stopped, startled by the noise.

Alice, seeing her sister was frightened, did a wonderful thing. She ran across the room and threw her arms around her sister and said, "Don't worry, I'm right here." Isn't that the way God does for His children each and every day?

He knows it's going to be difficult and that we're going to be afraid. We're going to be absolutely terrified at times of what lies in front of us. God knows we are blind. He knows living by faith and not by sight doesn't come naturally.

But then, "Believing is seeing."

chapter 35

AWAKENING LAZARUS ... SEALING JESUS

JOHN 11:45

"Many of the Jews which came to Mary, and had seen the things
which Jesus did, believed on him; but some of them went their
ways to the Pharisees, and told them what Jesus had done."

WITH JOHN, A story is never *just* a story. John leads us closer to Calvary than any of the Gospel writers. This strange man of Galilee has gripped John's own life, and he has no choice but to share.

John's account of the raising of Lazarus sets the stage in his Gospel for the events of that week. His version of the triumphal entry on Palm Sunday follows on the heels of the Lazarus story. In fact, it was the raising of Lazarus that electrified the Palm Sunday crowd, according to John. That's why the crowd was so big and boisterous, because of Lazarus and what Jesus has done to him, and with him, and through him.

It was that, in turn, that focused the Sanhedrin's opposition. They closed ranks immediately. The raising of Lazarus sealed the fate of Jesus, humanly speaking. The bringing back to life of one man assured the ending of life of another, and John is saying that Jesus knew it would be so when it happened.

A joyous, happy Palm Sunday ride into town for the people, maybe, but not for Jesus. The die was already cast and it was cast when Lazarus stepped out of the tomb.

But let's take a look at the way John writes his Gospel. We know that John is often saying more than he appears to be saying, so we always have to look for that. We know he often uses a particular story to tell a general story, uses a specific event to reveal a bigger truth. Nicodemus didn't understand; the Samaritan woman didn't understand; John almost seems to gloat in this confusion. We know he likes double meanings and plays on words. He revels in neat contrasts:

light/darkness,
    truth/error,
        life/death.

But one thing flows without change throughout his Gospel; he's obsessed with proclaiming Jesus as the Source of what's really important—light. "I am the light…I am the Bread of Life; I am the Way; I am the Truth." "Come and see." He invites, over and over. Every story John tells is essentially an evangelistic invitation.

The dramatic story of Lazarus may be the most intriguing, and, I think, the most touching of all.

Let's take a look at this story from John's perspective. It began with the news of an illness. Someone delivered the message to Jesus: Lazarus, His old, dear friend, brother of Mary and Martha, is sick.

What did Jesus do when he heard the news? What did He always do when He heard about a need? Remember, these were close friends; He'd been in their homes. He'd eaten with them, there was a special bond there. What did He do when He heard the news? *Nothing.* He did absolutely nothing. For two days He made no response at all.

What in the world was going on here? John wrote that Jesus stayed for two days longer in the place where He was. If He could drop whatever He was doing and go to the aid of total strangers, what kind of friendship was this?

If Luke were telling the story, or even Matthew, a delay like that would be totally out of character, but this is John, and this is a *sign* story, as the scholars like to call it. Jesus already knew what was going to happen and what the outcome would be, so there was no need to rush. There was plenty of time. The Son of God didn't operate according to the prompting and urging of others.

Jesus told them clearly, though they didn't understand, that something big was about to happen. The delay would only heighten the drama. What was to occur was for the glory of God, as John said: "That the Son of God may be glorified by means of it."

In John talk that means that the illness of Lazarus and his death and the dramatic aftermath of that, which Jesus and Jesus alone anticipates, is a fore-shadowing of what is to happen to Him. Of course, we now know that the raising of Lazarus will precipitate the Son's glorification, the Son's coming to glory, and that can only take place through the Son's own death and resurrection. *And He knows it.*

While the disciples were itching for action and thinking about tomorrow, Jesus was preparing for destiny and thinking about eternity. If we really stop and think about all that happened in this one story, this all-important story... We surely understand that this was not simply a family crisis in Bethany. It was a crisis of the entire human family, not merely the bringing back to life of one individual person, but the giving of life to every person.

Mary and Martha wanted their brother back, and so did Jesus, but at the same time He was acting to bring back life to a dying world possibly for the last time.

Throughout the Book of John are some of the most incredible and most repeated statements that bring solace to our lives, especially in the eventuality of death. Our ministers recite them at the gravesites of our loved ones. "I am the resurrection and I am the life. He who believes in me, though he dies, yet he shall live, and whoever lives and believes in me shall never die." Jesus said those words to Martha to console her.

But this funeral statement to Martha, for the first time, takes on a different "last rites" connotation. When He said, "I am the Resurrection and the Life," He said it as an invitation to something more. She believed in the Resurrection at the last day. She believed in something "out there" in a future triumph. He didn't offer her something less; He offered her something more. He offered her eternal life now, as well as in the future. Eternal life in John's Gospel was never just a quantitative thing, it was always a qualitative thing. And it doesn't begin at the funeral parlor, at the tomb, at the end of time. It begins with Him.

The Jesus who said, "I am the Resurrection," to Martha, the Jesus who wept with Mary, and the Jesus who drew Lazarus out of the tomb... so He could go in for our sakes...is by His faithful action, alive in the world today, *our world*, for those who will receive Him.

Faith is always first generation and only requires a hint of invitation to begin. God's been at this saving thing for a long time. He knows what He's doing.

chapter 36

THE GIFT

ACTS 2:2

"And suddenly there came a sound from heaven as of a rushing mighty wind."

Aᴜɢᴜsᴛ 24, 1992, was a very eventful date if you were living in Florida. It came out of the Atlantic Ocean, creating havoc in the northern islands of the Bahamas, pausing to catch its breath, and toying with the idea of veering northward, but then deciding a course directly westward was more to its liking.

It took dead aim on land just to the south of downtown Miami, and gathered all its incredible power for an onslaught.

The full force of the storm hit after midnight. The devastation was unbelievable. The mere scope of it defies comprehension. Mile after mile with nothing left standing; Hurricane Andrew had slammed into South Florida.

Story after story of the impact on people's lives began to filter through the media. The same words were reflected in anguished voices, *"What happened tonight changed my life,"* they said, nearly all of them… *"I know I'll never be the same again."* The winds of destruction had that kind of power.

But so do the winds of renewal. If I may be so bold, I consider Hurricane Andrew to be a negative example of Pentecost. The two events are different, of course. In some ways radically different.

Andrew was destructive; Pentecost was constructive.
   Andrew tore down; Pentecost built up.
      Andrew took away; Pentecost added.
         Andrew left people diminished and isolated; Pentecost left
            them strengthened and unified.
         Andrew brought fear; Pentecost brought hope.

You can explain Andrew, if you know enough meteorology; you can't explain Pentecost no matter how many "ologies" you've mastered. The two experiences stand in sharp contrast in some basic and fundamental ways.

Both represent an awesome display of power.
   Both came unexpectedly.
      Both underline the essential precariousness of the human situation.
         Both remind us of how vulnerable we are to forces outside of ourselves.
            Both make us aware that we're pretty puny when we are face-to-face with genuine potency.

If we could have been there to interview those present in the Upper Room at Pentecost, we would unquestionably have heard them say, *"What happened that day changed my life; I know I'll never be the same again."*

Luke tells us nothing about the behavior of the disciples after the Ascension nor does anything prepare us for the astounding events of Pentecost itself. Oh, they knew something special was about to happen. Jesus told them when He left, but they had no idea it would be like this.

They went back to Jerusalem as He instructed them; they waited, they engaged in prayer, they took care of a couple of routine administrative matters. They elected somebody to fill a vacancy on a committee...two candidates were put forward, their qualifications checked; speeches, I'm certain, were made. Somebody probably offered an amendment and somebody else moved the previous question on all that was before them...you know the drill.

Finally—gosh this is embarrassing—finally, they made the decision by means of a lottery...it just goes to show you how badly in need of outside help they were.

Suddenly, right there on the floor of the Upper Room itself, pandemonium broke loose. A Hurricane St. Andrew; that's exactly how Luke described it. A mighty wind whipped through the room. Tongues of fire reached out and landed on every head.

There was noise and commotion everywhere.

Now, when you really think about it, a Pentecost is scary stuff. Having the Lord on your hands is no tame experience to say the least. Paul Schere somewhere has written, "What if we stopped singing, 'Blessed Assurance, Jesus is mine,' and started singing, 'Blessed Disturbance, I am His?' Having the Lord on your hands—not the Lord of modest decorum and timid decency, but the full-throated and robust God of the New Testament.

Could we have measured the speed of the wind that day the way they clocked the speed of Andrew's wind? To think of it in those terms is to miss the point. We know enough Bible now to know how to translate those things. Wind and fire stand for God and God's activity.

Luke was saying God is bigger than our buckets, bigger than our labels, bigger than any of our categories and structures. We can't control Him and we don't program Him. After Pentecost, you never hear much about the church being closeted again in a little room. That mighty wind in a sense blew the walls down and pushed them out into the street.

I can't explain Pentecost any more than I can explain Creation or Incarnation. I don't think Luke could explain it either. I don't think he was trying to. He was writing filled with awe at the sovereign majesty of the Lord God of the universe, who by His grace acts in human life for our redemption, who acted here in a mighty way—and His key emphasis is not on the particulars of the experience, but on the results. It's what happens when God takes over.

J. B. Phillips wrote of his translation of the Book of Acts, *The Young Church in Action*, "It is impossible to spend several months in close study of this remarkable book without being profoundly stirred, and to be honest, disturbed." The Spirit does that. That's how you know the Spirit's been there. Maybe we can't specifically point to the explanation of Pentecost; maybe we can't define it, or account for it, but we can point to evidences of it. The Spirit may come without warning, but it leaves its footprints where it has been and those footprints take an *inclusive* shape.

Pentecost changed the character of Christianity forever, or perhaps it would be more accurate to say it formed its true character.

When the energizing winds of the Spirit blow, people can't help but be generous with their time, their money, their skills and their witness. The Spirit gets inside and you can't be the same anymore.

It happened to a group of followers over two thousand years ago, and from that day on everything was different.

"Suddenly, from heaven there came a sound like the rush of a mighty wind." Do you suppose...Do you suppose...

chapter 37

WE FINALLY HAVE HOPE

ACTS 4:12—13, AMP

"And there is salvation in and through no one else, for there is no other
name under heaven given among men by and in which we must be
saved. Now when they saw the boldness…of Peter and John…"

IN WORLD WAR II there was a German prison by the name of Buchenwald.
Even today the name sends shivers up and down the spine. All that was
horrible and ghastly, all that was physically and emotionally and spiritually
debased took place there.

At Buchenwald prison, a group of medical doctors were imprisoned, along
with thousands of others. Some were Christian, some were Jewish and some
had nothing at all in the way of religion.

They were thrown into the same compound with the rest, indiscriminately.
No distinction being made, no preferential treatment given.

Just like all the rest, the doctors were starved, beaten, and overworked.

But at night, when the others had dragged themselves off to bed, this little
group of physicians met and talked…They talked about medicine, they talked
about cases, they swapped observations and diagnoses, they organized within
the prison camp a little medical society, and did what they could to improve
health conditions.

Then they began smuggling in materials to make, of all things, an X-ray
machine. The parts and pieces had to be located, stolen, concealed, and carried
back to the compound.

It took weeks and there were all kinds of disappointments. But little by little
they did it, working for the most part into the night while others were sleeping.

They actually used that crude instrument in Buchenwald prison to help take
care of their fellow prisoners.

Dr. Karl Menninger, the famous psychiatrist of the Menninger Clinic in

Topeka, Kansas, tells the aforementioned story when he visited Buchenwald in 1945 after it was liberated. Dr. Menninger concludes that the one ingredient in the situation, the one factor that makes it not only possible, but plausible was the quality of hope.

These doctors literally never gave up hope.

Another story comes out of the hills of Tennessee. The Tennessee Valley Authority (or TVA) has been erecting dams since the 1930s for purposes of conservation and electricity. The water that backed up to create these dams and others flooded a whole section of bottom land turning some good, rich property into a lake. People lived on that land, called it home for many generations. Their fathers and grandfathers had farmed it for decades. But the government prevailed and the floodwaters came.

People knew that they had lost their fight, the battle had been won, and not by them. Their homes would be taken in the very near future by the water. Some of the people with relatives who had been uprooted still tell the story of the people's plight. Uncle Ephraim commented with native, untutored wisdom, "You know, when there ain't no faith in the future, there ain't no power in the present." I think Uncle Ephraim could have been an Old Testament prophet.

I think both of these stories are about the same thing, Hope. They just come at the point from a different direction, but they illustrate the same point, and they're about as solidly biblical as you can get. Maybe Uncle Ephraim said it a little backward, but truly, when there is faith in the future, there's hope in the present. Hope does that for us; it gives us something to cling to.

> As Christians our hope is not rooted in things,
>> it's not rooted in events or holidays on the calendar,
>>> our hope is not even rooted in the times. Our hope is rooted in
>>> God, and in His power to remain true to Himself…and to us.

I think if we can just believe that, then there is hope in whatever happens and there is motivation for "hanging in there."

The Gospels tell of two intrepid, bull-headed, spirit-intoxicated disciples who were hauled before the Sanhedrin on the charge of stirring up the people with their preaching. The authorities laid it out quite plainly before them. "Cut out this nonsense or else."

I suspect Peter and John took a deep breath, remembered Easter morning, looked the Sanhedrin officials square in the eye, and then said, "Hey, whether it's right to obey you or God is something every man and every woman has to work out alone. All we know is something has happened in the world that never happened before. Regardless of you, we can't help but speak of what we have seen and heard."

I guess there are some things in life that nothing else in life can touch. To put God first is to know hope. To have this hope implanted within us sets us free to look at the world around us with realistic eyes, because with hope, our destiny is beyond its control.

chapter 38

TO CORINTHIANIZE

1 Corinthians 1:2

"Unto the church of God which is at Corinth, to them that are sanctified in Christ Jesus, called to be saints, with all that in every place call upon the name of Jesus Christ our Lord, both theirs and ours."

Two hundred miles northeast of Los Angeles, California, lies a desert gorge which goes by the forbidding name of Death Valley. In altitude it's the lowest spot in the continental United States—276 feet below sea level.

It's the hottest spot in the United States. The maximum temperature reading is 134 degrees Fahrenheit. Practically nothing lives there. A few little rivulets run down from the surrounding mountains into Death Valley and just disappear into the sand. The average rainfall is only two and a half inches, less than we get in Winter Park the weekend of the art festival. I learned all this on the Discovery Channel. (Death Valley, not the art festival.)

Awhile back an amazing thing happened out there. It was completely unseasonable, completely unexpected, and completely out of character for that region of the world, but for some reason, it began to rain in Death Valley, and it rained for nineteen straight days.

Nobody in living memory had ever seen anything like it. Suddenly, out of nowhere, all kinds of seeds that had been lying dormant for years burst into bloom, filling the whole area with color and beauty. Those who resided nearby called it a miracle. In a valley known for death, people were surprised by life.

The Crucifixion is the Death Valley of the New Testament. It's the lowest spot on the biblical continent. It's the desert floor of the human existence, the end of the road. *Or is it?*

In the nineteenth century, parents in New York had a child who was extremely weak and sickly, even from birth. They did their best, they tried, they took him to the finest doctors, they worked with him, but he didn't get any stronger.

They lost heart; they gave up. They said, "He's never going to be strong and healthy. We might as well admit it." *They judged his whole life by his infancy.*

Some years ago there was a college student who bogged down in the sophomore slump. Most of us know about that. He was actually suffering from dyslexia, but that word didn't exist back then. He saw letters and numbers backward. He couldn't focus properly and his grades went down. He was right on the verge of throwing his books and everything into the trashcan and leaving school forever. *He judged four years of college by one bad semester.*

In the eighteenth century, a musician went deaf. His hearing deteriorated to the point where he literally couldn't hear it thunder. He thought he was through, thought he was finished in his work. He judged a whole career a failure because of an immediate setback.

Where am I going with all of this? Well, biblically it would appear that the disciples followed their master right up to the needle's eye of death. Then they saw everything, all their hopes and dreams, disintegrate in their hands.

They judged everything by the tragedy of the moment.

It's a mistake to judge too quickly. It's a mistake to judge a day by just one hour,
> or a year by just one day,
>> or a lifetime by just one year.

The frail child who looked as though he'd never be strong grew up to be a rough rider by the name of Teddy Roosevelt.

The dyslexic college student who was so disgusted with his studies and was on the brink of quitting had a renewed vision of truth and went on to do some rather notable work in the area of physics—Albert Einstein.

The musician who lost his hearing was none other than Ludwig von Beethoven who went totally deaf and wrote his magnificent Ninth Symphony, which he was never able to hear performed.

The cold, pallid darkness of Good Friday turned into the most radiant surprise this old world has ever known, and who would have believed it possible? *We just never know.*

Paul was probably a lot like these famous people we just talked about. He was just minding his own business one day sitting at the local Einstein Bagels outlet at the intersection of Damascus and Emmaus Boulevard, enjoying a latte and the next thing you know, he found himself in a crossroads town…the meeting place of east and west, the collision of hope and despair. Corinth had seen it all and offered it all.

The *International Bible Student's Manual* describes Corinth as a hard town, a coarse town, a town of thugs and extortionists, pimps and harlots. When you go there today you can still look up and see the Acro-Corinth, the high wall on the outskirts of the city on the top of which, in the first century, sat the infamous temple of Aphrodite, goddess of love, with its ten thousand temple prostitutes…at forty-three hundred denari each for four hours. The best customers came from the Senate chamber.

William Barclay points out that the Greeks had a verb, "to Corinthianize," said with a sneer. It meant to live like a Corinthian on a level sleazy and sordid, with little regard for standards.

This was what Paul was dealing with when he wrote, realizing that the Corinthian mind-set was present not just in the atmosphere outside the church, but that it had crept inside too, polluting the thinking of many within the congregation. The wonder is not that a church could flourish there, but that it could even exist.

In this type of atmosphere, Gnosticism became the word of the day. "Hasn't Paul told us about grace, that we're free in Christ? That means (doesn't it?) that if our souls are saved it doesn't matter about our bodies? We're unrestricted now; we can do as we please."

Some have said about Paul that no matter where you set him down, no matter what direction you turn him, pretty soon he's dragging Jesus into it.

"Do you not know you are not your own? For you were bought with a price." And there you have it… Those few words that are the building blocks of the New Testament. I think if you want to talk about anything that has to do with the Christian life this is the place to start. *Get the ownership business settled and the rest falls into place.*

When we finally understand that our bodies, our families, our church belongs to God, that the very breath that we take into our lungs, then it's easier to see that nothing we have—not even ourselves—is truly ours, but God's. These possessions belong to the God who bestowed them on us, and in whose honor finally may be used wisely and not wasted.

Paul wasn't just talking to Corinth or Rome or Galatia or Thessalonica. He was talking to us. I think we need to remember that the place where we worship is a building, built by human hands. We, the ones who enter the building, are the church. We bring the church into the rooms to gather for the purpose of worship.

We often forget that Jesus told Peter, "Upon this rock, I will build my church." We forget who the "I" truly is.

Paul challenged all his fellow disciples to *remember*. *Remember who and whose you are.* Remember where you came from. Remember the Cross. Remember what He's done for you. "You are not your own, for you were bought with a price."

Get the ownership settled, and the rest falls into place.

chapter 39

THE GOOD NEWS OF NEWNESS

2 CORINTHIANS 5:17

"If any man be in Christ, he is a new creature..."

JUNO...Sword...Gold...Utah and Omaha Beach. Many lives were lost that day, D-Day, June 6, 1944, when a countless number of Allied soldiers, sailors, and airmen made the ultimate sacrifice to establish a beachhead in the teeth of Nazi opposition. It was only the beginning, though. Thousands of additional lives would be lost between that day and the final end of the war, more than a year later, the day we now call VE-Day, Victory in Europe. The war didn't end on D-Day. There was still fierce, bitter, raging fighting to be conducted. There was still pain, suffering and death to come, for many...on both sides.

But from that day on to the signing of the armistice in July of 1945, the outcome of the war was assured. It was evident that the tide had turned decisively, that Hitler could not win, that the forces of freedom eventually would triumph. Their armies of totalitarianism were now boxed in, hedged about, tapped by the armies of the free world and though they could still wreak havoc, though they could still maim, kill, and destroy with fearful devastation, their ultimate demise was now only a matter of time.

Oscar Cullman, a New Testament scholar of the twentieth century, who was himself German (though not Nazi), has suggested that you can draw a kind of a parallel between these two polar events of World War II and the story of Christianity.

We're living today where evil still has plenty of power. The enemy still has the capacity to unleash enormous devastation on human life, still has the power to undermine, and maim and destroy, but the beachhead that will lead to ultimate victory has already been taken. Calvary is D-Day and the beachhead was secured at a staggering cost.

I don't feel that any human can fully grasp the agony, the pain, the divine

163

suffering involved in storming the hill of Golgotha to wrest once and for all the power of sin from the spiritual enemy. The full scope of it is simply too big for our minds to wrap around.

But it happened! That's the Christian story...that's the gospel. It means the old, crippling, stifling doesn't have to remain as the controlling factor over a life any longer. All that has been removed...if we allow it.

It's where Christianity becomes personal. "If anyone is in Christ, there is a new creation. Everything is passed away. Behold, everything has become new."

The Christian message,
    the Christian summons,
        the Christian call to discipleship is a call to transformation.

It's a call to a whole new reorientation of life from within—from the inside out—that's the call—and the Good News is that, in Christ, there is the power for that transformation to take place. Miss that and you miss the whole thrust of Christianity.

Once you acknowledge that Christ is the Son of God, your personal Savior and that He alone died for your sins and you have the *faith* to believe on Him, you lay your garbage at the foot of the Cross and you...*grow.*

I'm told they still tell the story at Princeton University about Albert Einstein. When the news came from Chicago that the first successful splitting of the atom had occurred, in that controlled testing that they had worked on for so long, conducted on the campus of the University of Chicago—when the announcement came by telegram to Einstein's lab that they had done it, that fission had occurred—they knew that they could make it happen again. They say Einstein climbed up on a table in the middle of the laboratory waving a telegram in hand and said in his clipped German accent, "Gentlemen, gentlemen, listen to me...now *everything* has changed."

Christianity is not about reformation; it's about transformation; a whole new reordering, reprocessing of what's deep down inside. Time has shifted its course, and so have you. Change has occurred and will continue to occur...in you...and me.

This new creation, this new reality, this new state Paul is talking about is not an achievement. Not something you did...it's a *gift*! It's *grace*. And it is offered to all who would accept it.

God's promise of transformation is not a demand: Clean up your act, pull yourself together, be kinder to your family…that's not it. That's a dead end.

It's always a dead end. Sooner or later Luther, Wesley, and Paul himself discovered this after almost killing themselves, trying to accomplish demands by willpower.

Demands, especially divine demands, just seem to pour more burdens on us, weigh us down with even more guilt. The more you do, the more you feel obligated to do. God's promise of transformation comes at it from a 180-degree directional change.

It's not a demand at all,
it's an invitation…
it's not a request to do something…
it's a request to let *Him* do something.
The result is not of something you do, but of something you permit to
  be done in you.
It doesn't deny us our humanity; it magnifies it.
It doesn't wipe out our identity; it enlarges it.
It doesn't take away from who we are; it adds to who we are.

Someone has said, "We are not human beings trying to become spiritual. We are spiritual beings trying to become human." I think that's it. That's the real truth about us. The purpose of the Cross, the D-Day event, is to make it possible for that to happen.

We are not really ourselves as long as we insist on living within a closed system. We are not really ourselves as long as everything we do, every experience we have, and every person we meet is thought of in terms of what this will do for us.

We are not really ourselves as long as we deny that inside us there is a deep, deep longing for communion with someone else.

In the second century, Irenaeus, Bishop of Lyons, said, "The glory of God is the fully alive human being." It's not far-fetched at all, nor is it limited to a few highly trained, selected, spiritual athletes. I believe there's nothing more down-to-earth than this.

The new creation is a process by which, over time—and maybe by fits and starts—we allow God access to the deepest yearnings of our soul, we uncover our hurts and wounds in His presence and let Him heal them.

And one day, before we know it...we are alive.

"If anyone is in Christ, there is a new creation. Everything old is passed away, behold, everything is new."

chapter 40

WHY?

JOHN 3:16

"For God so loved the world, that he gave his only begotten Son, that whosoever believeth in him should not perish, but have everlasting life."

WHY WOULD HE do it? Why would He bother? Why would it be important enough to Him to take that kind of daring, decisive, dramatic action on behalf of humanity? The creatures who from the start had virtually thumbed their noses in His face? *Why*?

The timing and location of the event is even more of a mystery. Why there? Why then? The location of it seems strange, don't you think? Born in Bethlehem of Judea, of all places, and of course, there is the *how* of it that sends your mind absolutely reeling. "Born of a virgin by the Holy Spirit." I guess the detail, the particulars, the specifics of the event seem somehow more manageable, even more fitting, when you begin to be grasped by the size and scope of the heart behind it all. If you can accept that there is a *why* to the story, you can accept the rest with relative ease.

You know we're talking about motive here. What's really going on behind the scenes, in back of the curtain. The result is the culmination of what we see in the rustic manger in Bethlehem. Believe me, it is rustic. I've been there.

My wife Sara absolutely loves a good detective novel or mystery TV program. The television show that she always watches is *Murder She Wrote,* with Jessica Fletcher. Throughout these stories, motive always plays a key role. In all of the detective shows that I'm forced to sit and watch with her, I have noticed that all the "stars" of the show spend a lot of time thinking about motive. Who stands to benefit from the crime? Whose position will be enhanced by the removal of the victim?

All of that is important stuff. If you know the *why* of the situation, you can get a better handle on the successive developments.

Isn't it the same at the other end of the moral spectrum? Actions, both good and evil, largely are the fruit of intent. Jesus obviously knew that. "Out of the heart are the issues of life," He said. "As a man thinks in his heart, so is he." He knew that if people wanted the right things, they'd allow those wants to lead them to the right choices.

You know, God has been working on this thing for a long time.

He's known what He's doing all along, what's been unfolding right
    here under our noses
        is not haphazard, or capricious,
            is not random, or reactive or frenzied,
                is not a matter of God being up against a wall and having
                    to do something out of desperation.

It's part of a plan, a calculated, worked-out plan. By a Master Designer, whose motive (and here I think we really and finally grasp the sheer wonder of it) doing all of that He has done was that He loves us.

In the book of John, the dreamer of all the writers of the Gospel expressed it in simple eloquence. He stated it so well, in fact, that it has become the best-known verse in the New Testament. I bet you are ready to recite right now before you read another word. You wouldn't be wrong if you called it the key sentence of the Bible. Certainly it's the verse that more than any other expresses as close as possible some kind of rationale to the motive question. "God so loved the world that He gave His only begotten Son, that whosoever believed in Him should not perish, but have everlasting life" (John 3:16).

Does this clear up the mystery? *No!* Absolutely not! Does it prove anything to the person who doesn't want to believe it? *No!* If you're not already tuned in, the verse by itself may not even be very convincing.

What if John has it right about this motive thing? What if love really *is* the force at the heart of the universe? *The church bets its very life on it!*

Did you ever wonder why God chose to come to earth in human form? After all, hadn't He already wrestled with Jacob out in the desert and appeared before Moses in the guise of a burning bush? Why a baby of all things? Why did He bother? I can only respond the way I know how. The church, through Jesus Christ, came to believe that God is not a harsh, cruel ruler anxious to pour out

His anger on mankind. His heart is filled with tenderness toward man and He has gone to the utmost cost in order to save man.

The fundamentally profound G.K. Chesterton offered this advice to prospective renters. He said the first question a renter ought to ask a landlord before even thinking of signing the lease, is not how much is the rent, or when it is due, or what are the accompanying amenities. Before you get into any of that, he counseled, you should ask your landlord, "What is your view of the universe?" For, he said, unless there's a belief in basic, underlying decency at the core of things, you can't expect to get much anywhere else.

Did you wonder, I mean really wonder, if the universe is basically benevolent? Does the One who runs it, whatever power runs it, care? I mean *really* care about these little ants crawling around down here?

The big question, of course, that comes out of this is the existence of God. Well, there it is, laid right out in the open. That's the question we want an answer to. What is the truth about what lies behind everything else? *Does* anybody care? Is there nothing out there but unfeeling mechanical precision, or is there someone, someone personal, who hurts when we hurt, who cries when we cry, who suffers when we suffer, and to whom what happens to us...matters?

The incarnation of the one true God answers that question with a resounding *yes*! And even if we can't prove it, we believe it down to the very marrow of our bones. Our faith hangs on to it.

God so loved the world that He came, that He identified, that He sent, that He *gave*.

John's song of love shows the relationship between Creator and creation. A love that does more than just exist in neglect, but takes the initiative to woo, to win the object of its affection, namely you and me. Love is always doing things like that. Can you explain love? No, you can't explain it. Why do you love somebody? Can you explain why? Really explain? You just do, that's all.

There is an unknown inspired writer in the Bible who, looking back over Israel's history thoughtfully mused over the "why" question when he wrote, "You are a people holy to the Lord your God. The Lord has chosen you out of all the peoples on earth to be His people, His treasured possession."

Are you ready for the answer for *why*?

He continues on, "It was not because you were more numerous than any other people that the Lord set His heart on you and chose you, for you were the fewest of all people. *It was because he loved you* that He brought you out with a mighty hand and redeemed you from the house of slavery."

What in the world kind of talk is that? "Set His heart on you because He loves you."

Maybe it doesn't make any sense, but it's the way love is, the way love does. It acts that way when the intensity of it builds up. And on one cold winter morning, two thousand years ago, God just couldn't hold it back any longer.

Writer Karl Barth expresses it in one asserting sentence: "While God's becoming man is not a matter of course, yet it can be justly considered as the most natural of all natural occurrences, because it was God who became man in Jesus Christ."

The One who makes absolute demands on us offers freely to give us entirely all that he demands.

The One who calls us to work out our own salvation comes Himself to give Himself so that this "working out" may take place in our minds and hearts.

Why would He do all that? Why would He care enough to make that kind of commitment? I can honestly say, I don't know. Maybe we should just blindly do what John tells us to do, and fall on our knees in grateful adoration.

There was an article written once by a plastic surgeon by the name of Dr. Richard Seltzer who tells the story of a young female patient of his for whom he was to perform a very delicate facial operation. The operation was imperative because of a small tumor that was growing in her face. To get the entire tumor, he had to cut away some healthy muscle and nerve. He was as careful as he could be, but the cutting just couldn't be helped.

He followed every natural curve of her face, but a tiny twig of nerve had to be severed, leaving her lips on one side twisted in palsy. She would live, she would recuperate, but her mouth from then on would be misshapen.

Upon visiting her room in post-op, Dr. Seltzer saw her husband there in the room attempting to give comfort and support to his wife. They were obviously a couple very much in love with each other. The young husband reached down to touch her gently.

Dr. Seltzer finishes the story in his own words: "He stands at her side on the opposite side of the bed, virtually oblivious of my presence. Together, they seem to dwell in the evening lamplight, isolated from me, private. Who are these people who gaze at and touch each other so generously and so greedily?"

The young woman speaks toward me, "Will my mouth always be this way?" she asks.

"Yes," I say, "I'm afraid so. It's because a nerve had to be cut." She nods and is silent.

The young husband smiles and says, "You know, I sort of like it. I think it's cute."

And all at once, I know who he is. It hits me, and I lower my gaze. One is not so bold in the presence of a god. Unmindful, he bends to kiss her crooked mouth, and I so close, I can see how he twists his own lips to accommodate hers, and to show her that their kiss still works.

In miniature form, doesn't this sound like the story of God's love, a God who bends down in unquenchable compassion to redeem His paralyzed world with a kiss?

"For unto you is born this day in the City of David a Savior, which is Christ the Lord." *He came for you and for me... He loves us because He loves us.*

NOTES

CHAPTER 1

1. Excerpt from Stephen Hawkings, *A Brief History of Time* (New York: Bantam Books, 1998).

CHAPTER 2

1. "Mark Twain Quotes," ThinkExist.com, http://thinkexist.com/quotation/man_is_the_only_animal_that_blushes-or_needs_to/215030.html (accessed March 16, 2010).

CHAPTER 18

1. Robert Browning, "Bishop Blougram's Apology," PoemHunter.com, http://www.poemhunter.com/poem/bishop-blougram-s-apology/ (accessed March 17, 2010).

CHAPTER 19

1. "All Creatures of Our God and King," by Francis of Assissi. Public domain.

CHAPTER 22

1. Frederick Buechner, *Whistling in the Dark* (New York: HarperOne, 1993).

IF YOU'RE A FAN OF THIS BOOK, PLEASE TELL OTHERS...

Write about *Looking At Life Through God-Colored Glasses* on your blog, Twitter, MySpace, or Facebook page.

Suggest Looking At Life Through God-Colored Glasses to friends.

When you're in a bookstore, ask them if they carry the book. The book is available through all major distributors so any bookstore that does not have *Looking At Life Through God-Colored Glasses* in stock can easily order it.

Write a positive review of *Looking At Life Through God-Colored Glasses* on www.amazon.com.

Send my publisher, HigherLife Publishing, suggestions on Web sites, conferences, and events you know of where this book could be offered.

Purchase additional copies to give away as gifts.

CONNECT WITH ME...

To learn more about *Looking At Life Through God-Colored Glasses*, please contact my publisher directly:

HigherLife Development Services, Inc.
400 Fontana Circle
Building 1 – Suite 105
Oviedo, Florida 32765
Phone: (407) 563-4806
Email: info@ahigherlife.com

If you would like a personally autographed copy of this book contact the author, R. Dale Perkins at:
dale67cubs@aol.com
407-467-1186